Lincoln's Secret Weapon

PORTRAIT IN OILS OF ANNA ELLA CARROLL

Lincoln's Secret Weapon

Winifred E. Wise

SOME OF THE AUTHOR'S OTHER BOOKS

Rebel in Petticoats
Jane Addams of Hull-House
Frances a la Mode

CHILTON COMPANY · BOOK DIVISION

Publishers

PHILADELPHIA & NEW YORK

To STUART

Contents

1

Golden Spoon

"And long may it wave!" The young lawyer-
poet, held temporarily prisoner aboard a British
warship in Chesapeake Bay, searched through
his mind for apt phrases and through his pockets
for scraps of paper and began to write it down.
Through the swirling mists of the early dawn he had been
able to glimpse the flag still bravely flying over the ramparts
of Fort McHenry. All through a day and a night he had
watched and listened to the bombardment; now by the
dawn's early light he could see that our flag was still there.

The patriotic pride which then surged through the heart
of young Francis Scott Key made the thoughts, the ideas,
the phrases come faster than he could immediately put them
down in words. Later he was to revise them and rework
them into a poem that—set to the music of an old song of
Revolutionary days—would become our national anthem.

To the tiny girl-child born a year later (August 29,
1815) on a plantation farther up the reaches of the old
Chesapeake, the flag and its stars and stripes was also to
become a symbol, and more than a symbol. Perhaps a passion. As the young, untried, only partially united United
States grew older and rolled with the passing years into the

1

turbulent currents leading to strife and division and to civil war, this girl plunged into the thick of things as no member of her supposedly frail sex ever had. One flag should wave above the ramparts, above the land—her land. Not two! Nor should "The Star Spangled Banner" ever be drowned in the swelling strains of "Dixie." "One nation, indivisible . . ."

Her name was Anna Ella Carroll. She was born into a patrician family that did not read history as much as they lived and made it. In spirit she always remained close to her famous kinsman, Charles Carroll, a signer of the Declaration of Independence. And when witty, cogent Ben Franklin said, "We must all hang together, or assuredly we shall all hang separately!" it was Charles Carroll who had added the defiant flourish, *of Carrollton,* after his signature. Carroll was not an uncommon name, and he had no wish to take refuge in any anonymity, nor to let the British mistake the identity of the richest and perhaps one of the most influential men in the colonies.

Even long earlier it had been Anna's great-great-grandfather, Robert King, who had ventured to oppose the mighty Lord Baltimore and finally to lead the Protestant Rebellion. All issues that are very dated now—but which were very alive then. The Kings had never lost their fire—and while Anna was still too small a girl to know or care—that branch of the family joined in a plot with Jerome Bonaparte in a vain attempt to set free his exiled brother, the fallen Emperor Napoleon.

The Carrolls, and most of their kinfolk, lived vividly for the most part; some of them within the narrow patterns of plantation life and some others spreading like quicksilver through the quickly emerging history of the country. It was, from where they saw it, a sort of tidal estuary of a family. Like the creeks and estuaries of the eastern shore of Maryland where Anna was born, everything was interlaced with some other stream and some other tributary—in Virginia, in Pennsylvania, and even up into the North.

The christening of Anna, the firstborn child of young Thomas King Carroll and his girl-bride, Juliana Stevenson, was an event to be signally remembered—if not by the child herself. Relatives in blood and "kissing cousins" in effusiveness and affection converged that day upon Kingston Hall. The rich relatives came in their carriages with outriders, the poorer ones by stage or on horseback; money really did not count then, but family and connections did. The widespreading Carroll house with all its twenty-two rooms would hold all of them, and more.

Ebony cooks scurried about the huge kitchen, each with her secret store of old recipes passed on from generation to generation—and a pinch of this and a pinch of that, a dash of that, the "beat it till de spoon stan's by itself." Cookery on the eastern shore of Maryland was a fine art, a way of life. It was based on the superabundant wild ducks of the marshes, the glorious terrapin, the succulent crab and all the shellfish. Eating on the eastern shore of Maryland was heaven piled high on silver platters.

The infant Anna, crying now in the complicated ruffles and starches of her long dress with its exquisite French embroidery, was little, but the newest symbol marking a long proud line. The Carroll family was a fruitful one, and would continue. Marking the occasion of this christening with the indicated mint juleps and also toasting the infant and her proud parents with sparkling champagne, the guests and kinfolk nodded agreement. Nathan the butler and his liveried aides kept the magnums flowing and the glasses filled—the service at Kingston House was always par excellence.

Thomas King Carroll, the host and father, was already

proving himself worthy of his distinguished name. Scarcely twenty-one, he had just been elected to the legislature of the State of Maryland. And he was a man destined to go far; no doubt about it. He was a man to watch.

As for Juliana his wife, the relatives were not so sure. Not a bad choice on Thomas' part, but there were many who thought that her father had been an extremist. Dr. Henry Stevenson had been a devout Tory. And much later he had been one of the very first medicos to advocate and practice inoculation against the then dreadful scourge of smallpox. They called him "the Madman," and his elegant Baltimore home (also used as his hospital) "Stevenson's Folly." There were those who had scorned him and his newfangled ideas to their everlasting sorrow; even at the christening of little Anna, some ladies had to lower their veils when the sunlight struck straight into their patrician faces.

Nobody, however, could deny that Dr. Stevenson's daughter, the young Mrs. Carroll, was a real, natural beauty. Along with her wide blue eyes and translucent alabaster skin, Juliana had her crowning glory—a head of hair of so soft and glowing a shade of red that no touch of henna could ever account for it. Wizened beldames took note.

As for the baby girl herself, time only would tell. It almost always did, with the quality. And even if little Anna did not grow up to be a beauty, she would certainly affect an air. She would undoubtedly grow up to be mistress of some great plantation; she would, of course, at all times defer to the wishes or the whims of her husband; she would rule the Negro slaves wisely and kindly; and at the last she would be gathered to her ancestors with the appropriate rites of the Church.

Episcopal, probably, though her father was a Presby-

4

terian. This branch of the family seemed always to be getting tiresomely involved in religious controversies. It was perhaps just something to be expected, like death and taxes. Thus the oldsters—gathered around little Anna's canopied cradle, and some of them at least wrinkled as the proverbial witch—predicted and proclaimed the tiny girl's course before they descended the stairs to join in the drawing room for more gossip—and another sip of champagne.

None could see, at least none of the dear old beldames could foresee, that old Mammy Millie, advancing upon them with stout firmness to protect her baby's slumber, had the last word. And that she held the future in her warm brown palm—still the hand of slavery. With the invention of the cotton gin some years before, the institution of slavery had become firmly woven into the Southern pattern; just as up in the North factories and commerce were setting the design. Some great New England fortunes had been built upon the African slave trade, but slavery had never flourished above Mason and Dixon's line.

In that year of 1815, the institution of slavery in America was settled and secure. The South was convivial and pleasure-loving and essentially feudal, scarcely touched by the cold rigorousness of Puritanism up North, where there was too much preoccupation with salvation and with avoiding the Devil's wiles to get around to seeing human slavery for the real sin it was. Nothing, to the Puritan mind, was a sin until somebody in the pulpit officially called it so. And Southern society, complacent at the *status quo* and at the exorcising of the only devil it had recently seen (in the form of the British redcoats), was enjoying the happy pursuits of this world, with very slight concern for the next. Riding to hounds took precedence over almost everything else. Could the famous and elusive fox, known familiarly in his own areas as "Old Red," be run to earth or cornered

5

for the kill at the next hunt, or would the wily creature continue to elude them, suh?

Anna Ella Carroll had been born with a golden spoon in her tiny mouth, but she had also been born at a time when it was really the last of the golden era for Tidewater aristocrats. Her name was like a hallmark upon the best and most luxurious of everything in this quarter of the world. Her father had recently fallen heir to a plantation of some two thousand acres, and his hundred and fifty slaves (many of them over six feet tall) were known as the strongest and the finest being raised anywhere. Lined up along the imposing avenue that led to the mansion, dressed in the green and gold livery that was brought out on state occasions, they were a princely retinue.

Outside now, in the slave quarters, the Negroes joined in the spirit of the christening celebration—"Juber will and Juber won't, Juber up and Juber down—we got the bestest gal in town!"

Far into the soft Southern night the banjos strummed. Slap-slap of hands and the shuffle of bare feet. "We got a baby bes' in town!" A party at the big house always meant one down in the slave quarters too. "She got han's and she got feets, lemme tell you! Suh, she caint be beat!"

Stealing away from the merry guests in his drawing room, Thomas King Carroll went upstairs to look again at the slumbering infant, his face in the soft candlelight touched with pride and yearning. She was somehow hard to believe in, this first child of his, this tiny stranger too fragile to be touched. The lovely Juliana had given her to him as she might have offered him a flower, rich and soft as the scent of roses that drifted in through the night.

Young Massa was a powerful "curyus" man, Mammy Millie observed from her watching post. He was a real deep one, though. Rising up, the old nurse spread her apron wide, shooing the proud young father away. "Go long wid you, Masser! Out! Ah ain' having you wake ma baby."

Millie's capacious bosom had opened to receive this mite of a girl, and now protectively enclosed her—as years before she had also enclosed Juliana. Little mistress Anna would naturally go the way of quality white folks; they still needed darkies to take care of them. White folks had ancestor pictures in great gold frames, portraits that looked proudly down upon the gleam of polished wood and silver and everything else that spelled tradition. Black folks had pictures too, graven deep in their minds. They were pictures that no one could care to look at or remember— pictures of men and women in chains, packed spoon-fashion, sweltering in the stuffy, stench-filled holds of the Atlantic schooners aboard which pious Yankee skippers held prayers every Sunday, and dropped overboard dead captives on Monday. Tales had been told, and memories lingered.

But life for the "Nigras" was basically good at Kingston Hall, even if the shadows and the sorrows were always in the background. Little Anna Ella Carroll went to sleep night after night listening to the wistful, haunting beauty of the Negro spirituals, to the soft rich voices singing "Deep River," and "Swing Low, Sweet Chariot, comin' fo' to carry me home."

2

The Old Plantation

Outwardly, at least, the white folks, the quality, were as sure of themselves in those early years of the last century as they were sure of the everlasting, incoming tides, the inevitable change of seasons, and the fertility of everything. Including the seemingly inexhaustible fertility of the "Nigras," ranging in color from blue-black ebony to the "high-brown" bronze, who bore their young to suckle like the lambs and the foals. Nuzzling at a Negro mammy's breast alongside a black child, Anna Ella Carroll fought for the rich, abundant milk that seemed ever to flow for her and for little black Leah. Heiress and slave child, they were equal. At least they were equally hungry infants; neither knew nor cared that one little girl was to grow up to be the mistress and the other to serve her.

For little Anna it was a time of absolute equality. Soon she was toddling around the yard with Leah and with the other "chilluns," and tumbling around with the hound-dogs and the kittens. They were, for that time at least, all young together. On the lovely moonlight nights, when most of the men, white and black, went out on 'possum hunts or sat over a jug of white corn liquor and listened to the dogs after the elusive fox, the girls back at home heard the puppies whimpering with excitement in their kennels. Perhaps little Anna, turning in her sleep, half-woke, and cried for dear Millie.

Millie was a refuge too, as far as Mistress Juliana was concerned. Millie had followed Juliana Stevenson from Baltimore to Kingston Hall. It was not too easy for a city-bred belle, a Stevenson daughter, to become suddenly the head, or at least the feminine factotum, of a great plantation.

And besides, now Juliana was soon to be once more a mother. Thomas King Carroll had courted her while he was still studying law in Baltimore. Suddenly, at the death of his grandfather, all this responsibility had descended upon the young couple. Juliana had faithful Millie and a number of other Stevenson slaves that had been given to her as a dowry or wedding present; humans in bondage were still her dearest treasures. So she brought them with her to Kingston Hall.

Unused to country or to plantation ways, Juliana had been suddenly forced from her brief honeymoon into the patterns and complexities of old plantation life. She had scarcely had time to adjust to marriage when she was called to take over Kingston Hall and all its complicated domestic arrangements; the ways and inter-ways of real plantation life of the time. It was a large assignment; without Millie, who knew everything about everything and everybody, it would have been impossible. The complexity of the domestic arrangements for 150 people! Without the thoughtful, know-how Millie, this all could easily have overwhelmed the fashionable doctor's daughter from Baltimore.

Juliana had a high responsibility. If the slaves, the owned people, were troubled, it was to her that they turned. And naturally, at the ripe old age of twenty, the young mistress

9

had not the wisdom of the ages. Yet everybody on the plantation had to be clothed and fed; and, like dependent children, they had to be trained for their appointed tasks. It was old Millie who—with her ear to the grapevine that led from the big house to the slave quarters—made a great many of Juliana's decisions for her and acted as a sort of counselor and chief adviser.

Millie knew how black folks thought, and usually she could read white folks' minds when it seemed indicated. She had the sort of wisdom that comes not from books (Millie had never even been taught the letters of the alphabet); she read *people,* and hers was the language of the unspoken word, the side glance, the innuendo.

So Millie was a Rock of Gibraltar, at least for Juliana at Kingston Hall. The lovely young bride-mother moved graciously among the sculptured gardens of the formal estate, among the white calla lilies of the plantation gardens. To tiny Anna, the small and very inquisitive child who had come so soon to bless this early marriage, her mother Juliana was a Being, extremely unapproachable. Mother was someone who bent over one's crib at night, with a whiff of fragrance. That was it!

Sometimes Anna, carried perforce to one or the other of the great balls and parties which the gentry still maintained, may have been allowed to peek down the great curving staircase and to have a glimpse, at least, of the fairyland of the grownups. Perhaps, with her young eyes dazzled by the candles and the crystal chandeliers, she failed to see her own father and mother there in the assemblage, and burst into tears. Social life and all its ramifications began rather early in the South; it is permissible to imagine that little Anna soon took a dim view of it.

She was plain, at least then, and she had what was called "carrot hair"—hair which, like her mother's, was later to be one of her crowning glories. But Anna also had, all her life, the temper which is popularly supposed to go with red hair. She took little or nothing from cousins or other compatriots who shared the same big bed. As a last resort, she called for Millie, who would always rise from her cot and come in and make sense.

Next to dear Millie, Anna was always closest to her father. Though she was his only child for a brief while, it was always Anna who was closest. It was this little redhead who managed to fill, in a certain very essential sense, the long empty cave of his essential loneliness, as even Juliana could not. Grave beyond his years, Thomas King Carroll was, even in his early twenties, faced with many problems. He had never before been in control of anything, and now he was in absolute control over a great plantation. He was a gentleman born; his appearance, according to the records of the time, was distinguished. But it is also possible that certain parts of this early dignity were only a cover up for the inward uneasiness that the present state of Tidewater affairs caused in him.

The years with his grandfather, an embittered old man, had left certain scars. The gaiety and the fast persiflage of Southern society required Thomas at times to retire to his study, to his haven of refuge.

Innocent hostage of the long-standing feud between Protestants and Catholics in Maryland, he often found himself upon the horns of a dilemma. He himself had been in a way the product of defiance. Thomas's mother had married a Roman Catholic, and had never been forgiven by her family. As an only child, she was the sole heiress to Kingston Hall, but she could never have it. Her father vowed that the place would never come to her and then fall into the hands of her husband who, under the harsh and inequitable laws of the time, would have property rights. A

11

married woman then had no more legal status than a slave; she could own nothing, and all belonged to her husband.

If she wished her line to inherit, she must give up her first-born son. Thomas King would raise the lad away from "popery's gauds" and introduce him into the strictness of Calvinist doctrine, make him high-minded.

Taken from his mother before he was six, the little Thomas had only remotely known her gentle influence. There were no sisters to soften the regime as stern old Thomas King, night after night, lectured to his grandson. Sitting by the fire, in a chair too large for him as it was too large for his grandfather's grandiose precepts, the little boy heard only endless discourse on Calvinism, politics, and law.

This was the only way to bring up a child—as a small adult. At least it was all that Anna's father had known. Taking his beloved little daughter into his lap he read to her no nursery rhymes, but strictly Shakespeare.

> With sweet musk-roses, and with eglantine:
> There sleeps Titania some time of the night,
> Lull'd in these flowers with dances and delight.

Enchanted with these cadences, Anna tried sometimes to repeat them in her childish voice. She did not know yet that few little girls of her time had ever heard that "all our yesterdays have lighted fools the way to dusty death." Loving her father's attention, stern though it may have been, she would listen even when she did not understand. "There's a divinity that shapes our ends. . . ."

Sometimes, Anna would climb with her father to the cupola that topped the big house, where, from the platform, he could watch the Negroes at work in the fields, tilling the corn, chopping the cotton, binding the grain into sheaves, and tending the young tobacco that was the chief money-crop.

The shadows beneath the distant chestnut trees could be the groving cattle, or they could be the Negroes napping. Young Mr. Carroll sighed; he had far more slaves than he needed to work the plantation, much of it worn-out land. Tobacco drew heavily from the soil, and the original riches had not been replaced. Scientific agriculture in those days was almost unknown, and a substitute for it was moving on to the west. The country was so large and abundant that few Tidewater planters even considered how to save the riches they had.

From this high viewing post, even little Anna could see the white sails of ships that seemed to float across the earth as they found their ways among the low meadow channels of the upper Annemessex. The waterways led to the wonderful world outside which, to a small girl's mind, could be only slightly larger than the domain she was already exploring at Kingston Hall.

Whenever Anna could evade Mammy Millie's watchful eye, she was off and away to watch Saul the blacksmith shoeing the horses, or to absorb the fragrance of the great tobacco barns, where the sunlight filtered through the chinks and the breezes crisscrossed and whispered secrets among the rustling leaves.

If Anna were polite and remembered to ask first, Auntie Susan might give her some warm milk fresh from the cows, or let her lick the spoon that ladled cream, or even stick her little finger in the butter churn. Sometimes—as briefly as one of the yellow butterflies that filled the air like flowers—Anna would settle down upon a stoop beside some ancient crone at her spinning wheel, usually with corncob pipe in mouth.

Kingston Hall was indeed a little world of itself, little touched by the sloops that came sometimes up the Bay from England or France. The Hall made its own shoes, wove its own cloth, raised what it ate and, except for wines and silks and velvets, needed little from outside.

Anna was a busy, inquisitive child, as inclined to roam as the sweetbrier roses that fell across the country lanes in wild tangles among the Queen Anne's lace. She did not fit in with the clipped hedges of the formal gardens of Kingston Hall; and, with her sunbonnet usually falling to her shoulders, she was Millie's despair. Sewing the bonnet firmly under little Anna's chin, Millie firmly admonished her. No lady, however young, should have freckles!

Importantly jangling keys large and small to fit every cupboard in the household, Anna sometimes chose to carry them all in a small basket and to follow close at her mother's heels. Cupboards were for locking against the overeager fingers of the "Nigras"—and also for opening daily to supply the household with sacks of flour, salt, medicines, and bolts of cloth. The seamstresses must always have their homespun, with a touch of city calico for more festive dress; the aged, their liniments. And the new dark babies, arriving in their usual profusion, their blankets.

Juliana, now close to her next confinement, must have sighed. There seemed to be no end to the babies, nor to her duties as mistress of Kingston Hall. Like her husband, she was beginning to feel the weight of a very large family, black and white.

Juliana was at the controls of a vast machinery, delicate in the exact balance of its human relationships, which could easily come to a stop at any moment. Now Uncle Nathan was insisting that the new houseboys, recently promoted from the fields, must go back to shucking corn. They were good for nothing better, the old major-domo insisted, jealous of his position as butler and of the years of service which had made him a ruler seldom disputed, at least in his special realm.

Auntie Dinah, the cook, had "sweet-talked" the "Mistus" into giving her mischievous grandsons a try, and Nathan wished to embarrass her. Soufflés would fall, the famous sauces would be famous no more, puddings would scorch. Unless Juliana could find some way of placating both parties, the whole population of the plantation would take sides in the quarrel. Diplomacy and manipulation—those were the necessary arts of the Southern gentlewoman. And as Anna grew up, she would learn those well!

3

Cruelty Up the Creek

As the great estates of the Tidewater country passed from hand to hand since colonial times, and the mansions mellowed with the years, still the gracious way of life had changed little from the earlier America, when most gentlemen were farmers. During Anna's childhood, it was inconceivable that this way of life would ever disappear, or that the inflexible hand of the past would temporarily burst the nation into bits.

The merry little Anna, her laughter echoing through Kingston Hall and through the well-kept slave quarters, was luckily unaware that the time would come when these walls would be open to the bats and the birds, and that even the stately boxwood hedges of the Hall would be destroyed. And, like the mansion itself, Anna's place in history would be long neglected and forgotten—until researchers, such as Marjorie Barstow Greenbie and her husband Sydney, delved deep to bring it to the light and burnish it.

Slavery could not forever endure in a land where "All men are created equal." Yet Thomas Jefferson, writer of the impassioned phrases, himself owned slaves, and freed them only with his death. The same had been true of

George Washington. The fathers of the country, the rich and influential, all had counted slaves among their assets; and few had ever paused to consider the Declaration of Independence as a formal paradox that was bound to pose questions that only the future could answer, if answer there could be.

Slavery was part of the American inheritance; and, to conscientious men such as Thomas King Carroll, it was already causing its perplexities. Above all else, a true Southern aristocrat had to live with honor; he had to meet, or try to meet, his obligations to the slaves born on the plantation and part of the family, for good or ill. With the final ending of the slave trade from Africa early in the century, and with the promised money to be made from growing cotton in the newly opened lands to the west, here were heavy pressures placed upon the older plantations to provide the human labor.

Sorely tempted by offers as high as $1200 for able-bodied slaves, some planters in Maryland, Virginia, and the Carolinas were yielding to them. Sad cases of men torn from their wives and families, and of women clinging desperately to their babies; of men being dragged across the mountains in chains. The backbreaking work in the cotton fields would exact its cruel toll; in five years most of the workers would be dead.

Yet to the Carrolls and hundreds of the gentry like them, it was unthinkable to betray the helpless beings intrusted to their care. Human souls and bodies could not be sold like horses or cattle, nor could they be treated brutally. There were not many Simon Legrees in the South, *Uncle Tom's Cabin* notwithstanding. A Southern gentleman might foolishly gamble away his family fortune at cards or at the races; he might even have a high-brown mistress and innumerable half-caste children; he might be ruthless to his wife. The aristocratic code did not ostracize him unless he practiced cruelty toward his slaves, or associated with the slave traders who were beyond the pale of this closely linked society. The planters shunned them, as a coarse and evil horde.

Plunging ever more deeply into indebtedness on plantations no longer flourishing nor able to indulge the extravagances of the past, still many of the masters refused to stoop to extricating themselves from their financial stress by selling off their devoted servants. They would rather sign more notes at the bank, mortgage their estates to the hilt, and run the risk of foreclosure. Others, unable to face fact or to continue to support a growing burden from which there seemed no easy escape, freed their slaves, and left them to shift for themselves.

So long removed from primitive life in Africa, the "freed" Negroes were almost like tamed birds suddenly released from their cages, and almost as helpless. With no money, with only the clothes they had on their backs, and little or no hope of any immediate employment, some of them stole whatever they could from nearby plantations; some built huts or lean-tos in the thickets along the creeks and tried to stay alive by fishing and hunting. Having been accustomed all their lives to being directed and fed and clothed by the master, many of them were pathetic prey for the predatory gentlemen out to trap them and usually to send them off to another bondage in the cotton fields farther south or west.

The law, controlled in part by the slave traders, might and sometimes did confiscate or lose "the papers" that declared these people freemen. Or Patty Cannon and those of her ilk might kidnap them.

Patty Cannon was a *haint*—waiting out there somewhere to pounce on Negro children who strayed around after dark;

she was supposed to be able to hoot like an owl, able to ride the wind like a witch on a broomstick. Old Uncle Fortune, telling stories to the youngsters clustered about his cabin door, spinning the old yarns about Br'er Fox and Br'er Rabbit, might now and then pause to listen to the phantom horse's hoofbeats along the lonely road past Kingston Hall, and to say, "Thar she is, chillun. That's Patty Cannon, out to git you unless you mind your mammy."

Anna, listening there with little black Leah, was certainly troubled later by nightmares; perhaps she shuddered when the people of the plantation (black and white) heard that Patty Cannon and her insufferable gang were out on one of their raids. Because Patty Cannon was not just a "haint" —she was a real person, a renegade Englishwoman of whom hideous tales were told, most of them true. She made a practice of robbing most of the travelers who stopped at her inn, murdered them in their sleep for what money they had, and also captured and hid Negroes in the attics of old deserted houses, starving and in chains, until she could ship them off to the West, or "down the river."

She had even been known, according to the records, to have beaten little colored children over the head with leaden whips, and once to have thrown a little boy into the fire to burn him alive. Some of this may be pure hearsay; but Patty Cannon was not a fictional witch. She did her evil, as far as she was able, until finally she was hanged.

Older than her actual age—at least sometimes—Anna Ella was necessarily sensitive to forces far beyond her immediate childish comprehension. Whether she would ever become a real Southern belle was a question far more important for visiting relatives to ask. She herself would not dance for them, nor show off for them in any way unless she happened to be in the mood for it; and even when she was expected to curtsy, she might sit tight and sulk. Examining her for the conventional features of a true Southern belle, the grandames did not yet find grounds on which to decide. Anna was freckle-faced and carrot-haired. Only a few of the old ladies, whom she preferred, saw the radiance of her smile—and it was unforgettable.

And it was almost always Anna who stood out among the sisters who followed her in rapid succession. The family resemblance between the Carroll girls was strong. Fire-red ran through their hair, in flames of varying intensity, the eyes were blue or gray but candid, the complexions fair. The Irish Stevenson strain was evident in their appearances and in their tempers, and all this seemed to be heightened and intensified in Anna Ella.

Beside her, the other sisters seemed weak and insipid. Taken alone, each of the girls had her accomplishments. Ada had inherited mother Juliana's gift for music; Julie was a young artist; Henrietta showed exceptional skill at needlework—and so it went through the lot of them.

But only Anna had a real interest in the learning that came from books. The other girls were being educated in "the three R's" and later would achieve the so-called elementals—a smattering of French, a mild and graceful facility at the piano, a few songs for a repertoire. Beyond sewing and embroidery, this was about all the education young gentlewomen of the early nineteenth century were felt to require. The further social graces, and not book learning, would fit them for their presumed future roles in life.

None of the other Carroll girls had the run of their father's library—nor cared for it. Thomas King Carroll was often away from home, from the plantation. But daughter Anna, by reading the heavy tomes, could bring him back close. Besides, her father would expect a full report on her reading whenever he came home from the sessions of the legislature in Annapolis, and his assignments were apt to be far beyond the scope of their gentle governess, who had a smattering of French and English history and a bit of Latin.

Her littler sisters could not imagine what Anna saw in these heavy tomes, these abominable volumes. They had few pictures, or none at all. Books then published and illustrated for children were little known, except for the ones designed to teach them moral lessons, in a drippy fashion the girls could not help finding drear. There was no pleasure for them whatever in books, except to throw them down and run outdoors to play, or beg for dance tunes.

Yet Anna, her young imagination fired by her father, was already interested in the law. Her father had marked places in the big books where she might read about the laws of the nation and of the state, and she sat conning the heavy paragraphs hour after hour until her little head began to ache. The words were long, the language strange. What actually did *habeas corpus* mean, what was *locum tenens,* and what was a subpoena? Laboriously, Anna copied down a list, hoping that someday her father would explain it all in one of his stories.

While Juliana might feel inwardly that this was training hardly suitable for a girl, she was not one to try to override her husband. And he took so much joy in Anna, the first-born!

While Thomas King Carroll was holding out to little Anna intellectual garments several sizes too large for any child, Anna could get into a sleeve here, a waistcoat there. She could picture him working upon the laws of Maryland, and sometimes catch glimpses of the men who had written the Constitution, and why. Her own father had known some of the founding fathers, had heard firsthand from them and from their sons and daughters of the bitter struggle to get all thirteen original states to adopt a federal constitution.

The heated days of this long battle were not old cold print in the history books to Anna Ella; they were living tales told to her by her father of brave and devoted men. Human beings did have a right to "life, liberty, and the pursuit of happiness"—and the Constitution protected them.

It was a new kind of government; a new concept that had thrilled the world. Despite their stuffy, formal words, this was what laws were supposed to be about—they were supposed to be about *people!*

4

Eldest of Eight

Busy with her own small pursuits in a corner of her father's study, Anna heard the gentlemen who came to see him arguing endlessly about "States' rights." Most Southerners, as her father explained to her when she finally asked, had never admitted that the Federal government, the one over them all in Washington, had more real power than a single state such as Maryland or Virginia or Carolina—and that it could override them.

"And what do *you* think about it, Anna?" Some of the visitors turned to the elfish, bright-haired child, looking for a moment of amusement. It was said that this precocious ten-year-old knew some of the Constitution by heart and could be persuaded to give recitations.

"I just don't know about these things," she answered them with a child's seriousness. "Wait until I'm grown up, and I'll tell you."

She must have been charming, sitting there with a pile of journals, cutting out pieces; probably she was going to make them into paper dolls, some of the gentlemen visitors thought. Patting her indulgently on her red head, the tycoons departed. And Anna's father helped her by picking up her clippings which had fallen from the table to the floor.

So many subjects, so many problems, interested Carroll! Lacking time to read all the newspapers and the journals, he had asked little Anna's help; she was to watch for letters and for articles about the new American Colonization Society. Thomas Carroll was active in this movement to help the freed Negroes by sending them to a place of their own— Liberia, in Africa.

Liberia was a new republic, recently founded by the Society as a new state for the free and for the freed. Anna was also told not to miss a single scrap in the periodicals about the Erie Canal, which had been recently opened as a new route to the west, and which was diverting traffic from the Chesapeake and causing outcries in Baltimore.

Anna's largest pile of clippings was usually about old Andrew Jackson, and it was here and now about him that much of the Southern press was again beginning to seethe with editorial rage. Imagine this rough, backwoods general and Indian fighter presuming to run for President! Didn't he have the sense to know that this was solely the right of Eastern aristocrats, such as the Adams family and the Virginia dynasty, and that no uncouth frontiersman need apply? Imagine a man like Andy Jackson striding into the White House with the red mud of Tennessee on his boots!

Jackson had been defeated once, and that should be the end of him. The South would continue to control Congress and the Senate, as it had from the beginning; and it needed no help from the West or North. Any true Southerner who supported Jackson was considered a traitor to his class, even to his people. Yet, as the record shows, some did.

And little Anna asked questions. "Is that right, Father?" she demanded, wanting to know whether she, too, was supposed to hate Jackson and all he stood for. As a child, even a precocious child, Anna Ella liked to separate the bad men in the black hats from the good men in the white hats; she wanted to take sides.

All that her father could say was, "Run along now, and don't bother your head about it." Yet Anna was still perplexed. Politics was an odd business if it even puzzled her father! He always knew what was right—only now it seemed that he didn't.

She ran down to the stables and asked for her saddle horse. She was suddenly tired of staying inside in the library and puzzling over the things that nobody, not even her father, could satisfactorily explain. So now, with the intensity she applied to almost everything she did, she whipped up her mount and took off. Anna could not remember when she had first learned to ride; leaping across log fences and over ditches with a daring that was certainly hardly ladylike, she flew across the country, or at least flew down some of the lovely lanes of Maryland.

It would certainly take a good deal of corseting and lacing, later on, to turn little Anna Ella into one of the so-called delicate flowers of Southern womanhood. The girl perhaps needed watching, but Juliana discovered that this one of her daughters could usually take care of herself. Preoccupied with the endless domestic details of the plantation and with her frequent and successive pregnancies, Juliana attempted little real restraint. Anna Ella was left unusually free to carve her own course in life, to wind in and out among the adults. Trying to combine all these grownup ideas with her childish ones, Anna went every-which-way, like the waters of a mountain stream dashing about the stones.

When it suited her, she read to her young sisters, often from the volumes of Shakespeare that her father so dearly loved. Draped in old velvet curtains, the girls would enact

25

the roles of kings and queens. Anna's favorite play was *The Merchant of Venice,* and as Portia she declaimed, "The quality of mercy is not strain'd!"

And then she added, perhaps,

> "It droppeth as the gentle rain from heaven
> Upon the place beneath."

If a woman could have become a lawyer in long-ago Venice, why should she herself not become one right here in America, in Baltimore? Why could not a woman have a major place in public life? Anna enjoyed playing at law, and, as the eldest of the Carroll sisters, she brought it into the settlement of girlhood quarrels. As the eldest daughter and presumably the ranking executive, she tended to take the role of both judge and lawyer and to pronounce the verdict in the solemn terms she had picked up from Blackstone and Sir Edward Coke.

And, sensing this native, latent power of analysis in this brilliant youngster, her father was doing his best to shape and develop it. It was Anna Ella who was the seldom-disputed leader in a family that would soon number eight.

Through the long languor of the Maryland summers, Anna left the books behind, and with her little sisters went sailing down the river to Chesapeake Bay itself, where Anna could see the clippers, with their graceful and rakish lines, turning back to home ports from the West Indies, or speeding out into the wild Atlantic under a heavy spread of canvas. Those schooners were the queens of the Atlantic, swiftest vessels on the face of the ocean.

The little town of Crisfield at the mouth of the river was known as the seafood capital, and here she peered into bins filled to the brim with shimmering fish and the harvest of crabs that, scrambling across blocks of ice, would be sent to markets as distant as Philadelphia and New York. Geography to Anna was not found in books but in clippers and crabs and in maps she drew with her father's aid to mark their route to other plantations.

Summer was the time for visiting, for spending weeks with other families, and for exploring new rivers and creeks with a party piloted by skillful Negroes. Rivers were not easy to navigate, and it was an art to anticipate the tricks of the currents and avoid the ever-changing snags and sandbars. Running aground, one might disturb a nest of snakes, and some could be the deadly water moccasin.

A particular thrill was going up the Pocomoke; it was like traveling through a tropical jungle, and one might imagine the lurking of strange and savage forms. For its narrow width, it was said to be the deepest river in the world. Cypress trees met overhead above waters that were sinister and dark, and a deserted mansion upstream was reputed to be used at times by Patty Cannon. One could see lights about the place at night, some affirmed, and hear the shrieks of murder victims. Anna would shudder and wish she had not come.

She welcomed the chatter back at the hospitable plantation, and dancing with boys who, already being trained in the manners of young gentlemen, bowed from the waist and asked for "the pleasure." Her father rarely accompanied them on these summer visitations, but Juliana was a social being who looked forward to them. Isolated for months at a time at Kingston Hall, she enjoyed the give-and-take of gossip such as she had known in Baltimore.

Such gatherings were a fluid form of communication between the widely separated plantations, and guests were in themselves like traveling journals. One might read political rumors in these columns, and trends of opinion along with the chit-chat. Juliana was on the alert for news of interest to her husband, and Anna also began to pick up bits and pieces along with the teacakes.

Anna found older folk interesting; and they, so often

ignored by girls of her age, were flattered by her attention. She was reading Kant and other German philosophers now, and it was amusing to hear her expound and ask questions. Recovering from the first shock of surprise such as might greet a dog that could talk, scholarly gentlemen listened soberly and did not mock her. Later, they might laugh about it all with their wives. What other girl of twelve or thirteen has so much as heard of philosophy?

As the summers slipped into fall and Christmas approached, Anna dropped her studies again for other pleasures. Christmas was the crowning event of any plantation year and the mark upon the calendar that divided it. One figured time as just so many months after Christmas or so many weeks before it. Well ahead of Thanksgiving, the Carroll girls were running about planning surprises and already getting in everyone's way. Anna and Julie conspired in one corner, Henrietta and Ada in another, while small Sally prattled and gave away secrets. Only the two boys, Harry and Tommy, were too young to care.

Would it snow this Christmas? Would mother like the slippers Henrietta was embroidering for her, and father the painting of a dog that bore small resemblance to his favorite retriever, though Julie had tried?

All over the plantation, the Negroes were working with a will to get in the last of the corn, to kill the hogs and make the sausage. The holidays promised a gay time in "quarters," and all must be in readiness. The smell of mincemeat and fruitcakes and plum puddings filled the air so deliciously that one could all but taste it. Turkey gobblers were fattening in their pens, and soon the great Yule log would be put to soak against the joyous season.

Every boat that drew up to the landing and every stage rattling along the road might bring boxes of presents; every post might bear news of more kinfolk planning to arrive.

In the North, the season's merriment was restrained by a Puritan chill, but in the South it had no limits as halls were decked with holly, pine, and mistletoe.

By dusk of Christmas Eve, Kingston Hall was teeming with guests; and the girls, exhilarated, were hugging even cousins they did not like. While the youngest hung up their stockings and were hustled off to bed, Anna and the older girls stayed up to dance the reels and quadrilles until exhaustion rang the curfew.

With cockcrow, the girls were all up again in time for the cry of "Chris'mus gif', Chris'mus gif'," outside their parents' door. As was the annual custom, a crowd of Negroes were jostling jocularly in the hall, each striving to be first with his gift to the mistress and the master. A brace of mallards, a prize terrapin, a barrel of blue points, a bit of knittin' or of whittlin'—whoever was first got an extra present.

The ceremony was signal for all the young folk to dress in holiday frocks and pantaloons. Arms loaded with gifts, they paraded through the "quarters" delivering these and caroling as they went.

All was high holiday throughout the week in the merry, merry State of Maryland. Anna's father, often so grave and distant with guests, expanded with the warmth of the season, kissed the ladies under the mistletoe, and made everyone forget that he did not care for foolishness. Ordinarily so high-minded that he froze the ripples of frivolity by his very presence, during the Yuletide he was the indefatigable dancing partner, the jovial host. What a shame, Anna thought, that the great Yule log must ever fall to ashes and that Christmas could not last all year. . . .

5 | The Governor's Daughter

Older than her years, and forced by her somewhat unique education outside the rainbow-
colored bubble in which most highborn Southern
girls of Anna's class led a light-hearted and
frivolous existence, she was already half a
woman, and perhaps half a man, in her thinking. From
clipping press stories for her father, she had somehow advanced into being his secretary. Though not yet fourteen,
she was already answering many of his letters and screening
the steady flow of visitors who came to advise him or to
ask for political favors.

Acting upon her earlier instructions, or perhaps on sheer
feminine instinct, Anna managed to shunt away the pompous
bores who echoed so hollowly with the rattle of their
verbiage, and to make time for those her father preferred
to see and spend time with. He liked to talk to anyone who
could give him solid information—the oystermen, the sea
captains, the small tradesmen. And to anyone who, by the
nature of his work, could possibly give him slants that were
fresh and were real. The times were changing, and Thomas
King Carroll sensed that the aristocratic class could hold

its place in society and in politics only by changing or adjusting along with them.

Most emphatically, he did not hold with the great John J. Calhoun of South Carolina, nor with the others who held the idea that "States' rights" were above the general good of the nation. Some of these men were already talking of secession. They were firm, rigid men, seemingly determined always to hold on to the past, where Thomas was flexible.

Like his aged relative, the illustrious Charles Carroll, who at ninety was backing the first steam railroad ever to open for general operation in the whole United States, this younger Carroll was turning his eyes to the West and to the future.

Aware of the strong forces from the frontier with which he had to contend, Carroll supported Andrew Jackson in his second try for the Presidency. Jackson was right, Thomas said; position and privilege must be earned, they should not be taken as an inheritance. He had made his personal, individual decision and could not be moved by the scorn of friends nor by the rage of visitors who pounded upon his desk and stormed, "No gentleman, suh, is a Jackson man!"

"My father will be what he likes, and do what he likes—and so will I!" Anna, hearing some of this commotion, burst through the library door. "No one called you, my dear!" Her father silenced her with a look.

Later her mother called Anna aside to admonish her. Anna must learn to control herself and her temper if she were ever to be of any real help to her father. In this curious world of politics, one could not say all he thought, Juliana explained. "Let the person across the table try to guess what cards you may have in your hand; it's a little like playing loo!"

Humiliated and tearful, Anna promised to try, again

31

and again. Both parents suggested that she had a tendency to go to extremes, but that was Anna's nature. All or nothing! She hated wishy-washy people who were neither one thing nor the other. "Precious Father," she would say, and then "dearest Mother," throwing herself into their arms in a passion of adolescent devotion.

The Jackson partisans were pressing Thomas Carroll to run for governor, but he had his hesitations. The battle would be a brutal one, he knew well. He would be a target for the filthiest of mudslinging and the most vicious of lies. Feeling was running so high at that time that rival factions were fighting with brass knuckles and eye gougers in the streets of Baltimore. Election to the state legislature was as polite and socially acceptable as riding to hounds. Thomas Carroll could linger there indefinitely, but he was ambitious and still young. So he made his move.

With Juliana cheering him on, he entered the race for the governorship. She herself would run the plantation while he was out campaigning, she said—trying to keep any possible uncertainty out of her voice. The family would all join him in Annapolis. Juliana had always wanted to live in the Governor's Mansion. Never mind about the new baby she expected, the eighth child. She and Millie would manage somehow.

Anna Ella, now flaming over what the journals were saying about her father, kept him informed to the best of her ability. She, of course, longed to be at his side during the bitter campaign, but Mother needed her too; Anna could feel that.

Father could win—and he did! The Carrolls would not go directly to Annapolis; Anna fumed at the slight delay but, as a planter's daughter, understood it. The spring of 1830 was, like any spring, a crucial time to leave the planting, the seeding of next year's crops to the hired hands of an overseer, or of anybody. Juliana must perforce stay to watch and direct in the necessary absence of the master; the Carroll fortunes at the moment were on a more precarious balance than anybody would care to admit right out loud in public.

Anna, writing out of sheer loneliness at home, said plaintively to her father that she had not been well. "If I had not the kindest and dearest of mothers to care for me and for us all, what should we do?"

Enough of complaints and self-sympathy. She was the Governor's daughter now, and, while still under the age of fifteen, his political aide. With an incisiveness that somehow combined the impetuousness of a child with the seriousness of an adult, Anna continued: "I understand that your appointments have not been approved—by the milk-and-water strata of the party, for certainly no thorough Jackson man would denounce. . . . It is my principle, as well as that of Lycurgus, to avoid mediums, that is to say people who are not really decided one way or the other. In politics they are the inveterate enemies of the state!" Here the ink spluttered from her quill pen. Anna was not one, even then, to do things by halves.

"I hear there has been a committee appointed to visit you on your return to The Hall, and present a petition for removal of same." Anna was even then keeping an ear to the ground, as her father had taught her to do. "They call themselves 'reformers.' I want reform too, even in court circles," she added with a slight touch of youthful flamboyance. "But forever to be reforming reform is to be absurd!"

The gubernatorial duties pressed on Thomas Carroll, and travel in those days was so slow her father could only promise them a visit. Anna must be patient; and her mother Juliana, weary of it all, was sometimes short with her daughter. Anna Ella was not the only one who missed

Thomas Carroll. Once the summer harvest on the plantation was under cover, the grain threshed, and the tobacco safe from mildew, they could make their autumn plans.

Baby Mary had her fresh layette, but still all the rest of the girls had to have new wardrobes. As the Governor's eldest daughter and at the ripe age of fifteen a young lady, Anna had somehow to be dressed in the height of fashion. Like her mother, she, too, must pass the cold critical eyes of Annapolis society.

Almost like a princess, Anna pranced sometimes before the pier glass, the mirror, in a rich blue silk that brought out the deep, subtle color of her eyes. Leah had laced her so tightly that the child could hardly breathe. Her new role in society had its penalties as well as its rewards. The tiny lace-bedecked parasol, the necklace of real jewels, the poke bonnet decked with feathers instead of the daisies of her childhood . . .

Princess Anna? That did not really sound well. Girls were always changing their names, from Flora to Florabelle and from Sarah to Samantha. The name of Anne seemed so much more distinguished than Anna, plain old Anna, and besides, it was truly the name of a queen! "Meet Miss Anne Carroll," Anna called to her mother. Watching from the hall below, her mother was watching her daughter's dignified descent of the stairs. The girl was handling her new finery quite well, but still she must be taught how to float in her petticoats and not grip the rail.

"So it's Anne now, is it?" Juliana laughed at her daughter's whimsy. "I must be sure to remember."

The younger sisters were now sewing, along with the plantation seamstresses, in the tiny, flying stitches Anna (or Anne) had earlier thought such a great bore. Anna did not care much for needlework, but the new Anne would try it. She would, as a magnificent gesture, make her father

34

a shirt! It must be easy; she had seen Leah do it a dozen times. Henrietta helped her to cut to a pattern, and no doubt giggled when one asked why bother with basting. Henrietta was as clever about sewing as her sister was about books. As she watched Anna-Anne's struggles with the shirt, Henrietta's voice was honey coated. Perhaps with sisterly sympathy.

Somehow all was accomplished in time for the triumphal procession up the eastern shore through the glories of the Maryland autumn. Princess Anne was riding in the front carriage with the "King" and "Queen," while the retinue of smaller sisters and brothers followed well to the rear, under surveillance. As Ann-Anna-Anne bowed to the crowd, to the right and the left, and, with her mother, accepted the bouquets of flower-blooms, Anne was still afraid that the rear was a signal disgrace. She knew it—by the hoots that indicated mischievous antics somewhere, right close.

Everyone had turned out—the innkeepers, the tinkers, the fishermen, along with the planters and their people, rearing on nervous steeds made more upset by the screech of the horns and the fiddles and the flutes. As suited such an almost-royal entourage, outriders, resplendent in the green and gold livery of the House of Carroll—went on ahead to arrange the nightly accommodations. Whatever his politics, a plantation owner in traveling was almost always overwhelmed by invitations from others of his social or economic group. It was a time when travelers had their problems; the inns were abominable, infested with bedbugs, and otherwise beneath consideration by the quality.

So the Carrolls took the journey of some seventy miles in fairly easy stages; but it was over far too soon to suit the younger Carrolls, shining as they felt themselves to be in all the excitement and resplendence reflected from their father, the sovereign of the state. Still, they were about to be ferried across the Chesapeake, and undoubtedly further adventures lay ahead of them. Anne, her hair now ablaze like an autumn leaf, stood at the rail as the ancient side-wheeler churned its way across the bright blue waters of the bay in the direction of Annapolis.

Long and long before they actually came to dock, she could see ahead, on a slight rise, the white cupola of the old State House where her own father had his offices, and where General George Washington had resigned his mammoth commission as Commander-in-Chief. This had been the seat of the new Congress of the then newly born United States of America itself! And Anne could hardly contain her desire to visit it; more than that, she could hardly wait to understand it.

As her feet echoed across the polished floors a day or so later, Anne paused perhaps before the glorified portraits of Washington, or of Lafayette; she fingered the tattered flags that the Maryland troops had carried through the Revolution. With a youthful ardency, she thrilled to the historic spot and hoped and wished that she, too, could somehow play a vital role in the story of her country.

But as far as she could see now, she was in for nothing but a long tedious term of polishing. Her father had several secretaries now, professionals who made her amateur efforts look quaint. And he, of all people, was now siding with her mother in the insistence that Anne attend a regular school—one that taught little more than manners, music, and French.

From Anne's viewpoint, it mattered little to learn how to enter a room or flirt with a fan. "Girls, don't ever raise your voices, keep them low and sweet." The elderly gentlewoman who ran the school (restricted to the daughters of first families) accepted Anne as a personal favor, of course,

36

just as she had the other girls. It would be hardly genteel to admit that she needed the tuition money.

In that perfumed and artificial atmosphere, the girls were taught how to blush, so that "dawn's rosy glow might creep across the pallor of one's cheek." They were receiving the finishing touches of an education not to be learned from books; it was the subtle Southern art of entwining men about one's little finger.

Pretend to know nothing whatever of serious subjects; if you do have a mind, conceal it, as a cat does its claws. Be quick at repartee. Turn away when the gentlemen press, but not too far. Be a living model of piety and virtue, yet on the saucy side. Know how to play the game of love so deftly that you can avoid getting caught up in the flames. A girl must remain upon a pedestal, to be adored from afar until at last, overcome by "the darts of Eros," she might swoon into the arms of her chosen cavalier.

Where years earlier Anne had been confined to the plantation with the long, monotonous drip of the winter days, she was now dressing for balls and cotillions. With her radiant hair done high on her head by faithful Leah, in a profusion of flowers and plumes, her skirt held wide by seven petticoats, Anne was moving, along with her mother and father, into her rightful place among the Carrolls, in a world of elegance and utmost sophistication.

Trying at first to hide the daringly low cut of her flowered silk ball gown beneath the folds of a gossamer shawl, Anne soon decided to throw artifice aside. Her white shoulders and arms were superbly molded, as even her schoolmistress had observed, and a lady must assess her beauty points and make the most of them. Her waist, of course, must be tiny. So, no chocolates. And she must further be laced and corseted almost beyond the breathing point! What a lovely swell of bosom a girl could achieve—unless she swooned and spoiled the whole effect!

Vivacious and mettlesome, Anne speedily became an Annapolis belle. She was soon mixed in a whirl of invitations for morning canters, picnics at noon, and saunters by moonlight up along the Severn River. The boys became a sort of interesting blur to her, and in early spring of that year of 1831 she was crowned by a fervent admirer as the Queen of Love and Beauty.

Romance showered upon her, like the falling of apple-blossom petals. The young men charged down the field, like knights of old in tournament, lances a-tilt, to show their skills and their manhood to their sweethearts. Anne's particular gallant of the moment won; she was the Queen. And how filled with rapture a Maryland spring could be!

Fall of a House
of Cards

Anne was caught in a spell of enchantment and hoped with all her heart it would never break. Why must she ever leave Annapolis, the first city she had known? Her father, as governor, had the official box at the theater toward which actors bowed formally at the beginning and at the end of each performance; one had the privileges of royalty without its restrictions. As in her occasional strolls to the pastry shop at the end of the street, Anne was tasting to the full the frostings on her cakes.

Yet houses were already being closed up against the coming oppressive summer. The ballrooms where Anne had danced with her retinues of beaux were being sheathed in the white of slip covers to protect the crimson velvet sofas and the Aubusson carpets, as the families departed for the cool, high air of the mountains. Anne had no real excuses to linger further in Annapolis. Mother had returned earlier to Kingston Hall with the younger children, and Anne must join her there. Leaving Annapolis wistfully, but with a fond hope of return, Anne did not guess that the book was closing on the gayest chapter of her life.

Back at Kingston Hall she was romantic and restless, as

39

might be expected of any girl of almost sixteen. The accustomed routines of home, dear as they were, bored her sometimes to tears. She wished that she could take off for Europe, like some of her classmates. Writing to her from Paris and from Rome, they were a world and more away from the Hall, and from the chorus of bullfrogs that Anne heard every evening. She too should be dancing to the music of exotic violins!

Impatient with herself and everybody after one of these gushing letters from a former schoolmate, Anne could not bear the fussiness of visiting relatives who had a way of upsetting the household routine by demanding breakfast at eleven instead of nine, or insisted that their bed sheets be changed every day. Small annoyances, perhaps, but they were large to mother, or Anne thought them so. Juliana had much too much on her mind trying to manage the plantation with father still away in Annapolis and Washington. There was now talk of his running for United States Senator, and he was getting steadily deeper in the nation's politics.

Anne, fresh from the capital of Maryland and with a new perspective, could sense a change. Kingston Hall was in some way uneasy, as she had never before felt it to be. She was growing up, and she could see more than she had.

Plantations around them were crumbling, but Kingston Hall would stand. It must! Thomas Carroll had not been using his heritage as a stake on the gaming tables, nor had he been pursuing beauties among the "high-yellow gals." Far too many plantations were passing into other and cruder hands, or even being deserted entirely to the blackberry vines and the Jimson weed.

The masters had grown soft with the ease of old plantation life. And now the creditors, in one form or another, threatened to engulf them. Not only creditors and bankers, but the ever-burgeoning crops of black babies that over-flowed the worn-out land. In the cycles of the seasons and of the years, Tidewater tobacco could not compare with the new Kentucky crop. Wheat was thin and hardly worth the planting and the reaping. But the notes signed at the bank could, it seemed, only be repaid by the sale of slaves to the West, or down the river.

Slavery was a hideous evil. Abolitionists in the North were only beginning to proclaim the facts of life that Thomas Carroll and other Southern leaders like him had long been facing; it involved a deep problem that many were trying in vain to solve overnight. Carroll and many of the other plantation owners saw the institution of slavery purely in the absolute terms of the individual black folk they "owned" and loved. What could they do to see that a hundred Mingos, Sallys, Fortunes, Millies, and their children and grandchildren were safe and secure?

Planters signed notes for each other at the bank in an endeavor to postpone the day of reckoning, and, still living extravagantly, pretended the day would never arrive. In reality, the burden had become so great that they themselves were in a way enslaved! At Kingston Hall alone, the original hundred and fifty slaves of Thomas Carroll's inheritance had almost doubled in number, while the work for them to do had almost as rapidly diminished. Unlike the factory owners in the North, the planters could not dismiss workers when times were slack; they could not turn their backs on the aged or close their eyes to hunger. The planters had never been truly rich, except in land, and now even this was failing them.

While her father was deeply engaged in large affairs of state and of the nation, Anne watched her mother trying to add up accounts that would not balance, and trying at the same time to maintain a hospitality that the Carrolls could no longer afford. Anne said nothing about her need for a new ball gown, and was a bit harsh when her sisters demanded new slippers or her brothers wanted boats. They must learn to manage with what they had and not always be bothering Mother. No! They were not going back to Annapolis, and please, please stop asking why not?

Juliana was pale and drawn. She had tried too hard and too long. She collapsed, dropping the reins. Millie as always did her best, bringing the hot flatirons for her mistress' feet, the smelling salts, and the herbal potions. But what Mother really needed was Father. Anne, as temporary head of the family, dispatched a letter with Mingo. But it would take days to reach him, and days for him to come. Still, it was the best that the young and worried girl could think of.

It had all been too much for Juliana; eight children and several miscarriages in too short a span of years. A husband whom she adored but who was often harsh, demanding, and difficult—who was expecting Kingston Hall to run itself. A crisis, inevitable and long in the formation, was upon them.

From the wide expanses of his dreams for the Senate and a great political future, Thomas Carroll *must* return to the narrow, outdated world of Kingston Hall to try to save both it and his Juliana. The house of cards was falling; these cards dealt from one gentleman to the next. Besides his own considerable debts, Thomas Carroll had rashly assumed those of others of his friends and *compadres,* for whom he had co-signed notes at the banks. As a man of principle, he would pay them, no matter what it really cost him and his family.

While the old plantation improved under his renewed, constant attention, the odds were against him and his ilk. True, food was abundant—food from the lush gardens tilled by the Negroes, ducks from the marshes, and the fish that teemed in the rivers and the Bay. What the Carroll family really needed was ready cash, and finally Anne herself suggested an idea—the idea of a school!

Kingston Hall had plenty of room for a school, and she would teach in it. With all the ardor of her youth, she was still somewhat vague about the curriculum, but what did that really matter in a finishing school such as the one she herself had attended in Annapolis? The faded gentlewoman who ran that school must have made pints of money —or so it seemed to Anne. And the old lady was not half so smart as Mother.

It was, perhaps, a harebrained notion. Both of Anne's parents dismissed the idea at first, and then later reconsidered. Juliana recalled letters from her friends in Baltimore, asking whatever on earth they could do with their daughters until the dear girls married and settled down? A genteel boarding school, run under such auspices as that of the Carrolls of Kingston Hall, might be an answer for them, and for the daughters of the newly rich Baltimore merchants. It would, perhaps, have what would be later known as snob appeal.

Juliana brightened at the prospect. She was strong enough now to teach music, piano, and voice, and as the daughter of a famous doctor, perhaps physiology. Manners would be part of the course; Anne, with her odd but surprisingly comprehensive education, could fill in the gaps with European history and Shakespeare. Anne, of course, agreed enthusiastically to all this. They would teach girls to use their brains.

Anne had never heard of Emma Willard, or of her Troy Female Seminary up North, where students were shocking their elders by learning algebra and Latin. Elsewhere, throughout the country, girls were still regarded as lesser beings, capable of little more than reading, writing, arithmetic, and polite accomplishments, or, on the frontier, the primitive domestic crafts their mothers had taught them.

Glimmering in the sunset of Kingston Hall, the school was a success. Horseback riding was a more popular subject than European history, but Anne could teach either one. She was no real crusader in the field of education; if the girls attended school only for a lark or a break in the routine of living, it was not important to Anne—as long as their bills were paid.

She was helping her family in one of the few ways then open to a woman. Still under twenty, she was prone to youthful vagaries which could make her forget which one of the group was supposed to be teacher, and which pupil. Juliana and Millie had them all under their figurative wings, and it added up to a chattering flock of embryo belles which no doubt sometimes drove Thomas Carroll to distraction.

It was, however, the sort of finishing school that almost all of the parents wanted; a waiting time until the girls could be signed, sealed, and delivered into the arms of suitable husbands. With the Carroll stamp of approval upon her, a girl of humble origin might aspire to be an aristocrat. If wealth could buy charm and presence, most fathers did not quibble at the cost.

Her name and her background—Carroll of Carrollton— were capital like money in the bank, as Anne was dimly beginning to discover!

7

Facing Facts

There were still so many facts of life to be faced, so many little sisters and brothers somehow on Anne's shoulders! With her mother still but a shadow of her former self, and with Thomas Carroll deeply depressed at the fading of his political future and of his personal fortune, Anne felt deeply the weight of it all—the weight of all the Carroll family tradition and its pride.

Just as the education she had received, mainly from her father, had forced her beyond the usual pattern of a Southern belle of the time; so now the ubiquitous and obstreperous Anne tried gallantly to assume a responsibility for her five sisters and two brothers, a sense of responsibility rarely, if ever, found in a girl of her age.

The Carroll family must keep up appearances so that the girls could marry well, and the boys prepared for medicine or for the law. While the real inner Anne scarcely fancied herself in the role of schoolmistress, she was happy now to be bringing money into the Hall and helping to stem the tide of disaster. It might all be just a small bucket poured into an ocean of debt—but from Anne's viewpoint it was better than sitting back and doing nothing at all.

Yet as financial ruin swept the country with the panic of 1837, the pupils of the Carroll school were one by one withdrawn. Fortunes far more secure than the Carrolls' had been of recent years were crumbling. Hundreds of banks had failed; thousands of businesses were in bankruptcy, and unemployment was rife.

It was all the fault of that roaring, radical Westerner, Andy Jackson—the conservatives were quick and eager to place the blame on him for everything. Locally, the banker appealed to Thomas Carroll and to other prominent planters; all made a last-ditch effort, but the times were out of joint. And Carroll went to the wall, as the saying goes.

The Carroll family now had to face the difficult, perhaps tragic, decision they had been trying to avoid. There seemed now no other possible alternative to selling at least some of their slaves to the dealers in human flesh who hovered about the vicinity like vultures. With their long, greasy, unkempt hair, their smartish goatees and their brutal faces, these men were to Anne subhuman creatures. They were predators. Ethically and emotionally this course would be devastating as well as infra dig; it would almost be the equivalent of selling the members of one's own family! But even despite the current depression, the Carroll slaves would still fetch a top price; they were among the finest and strongest in all Maryland.

The plantation, despite its two thousand acres, would never find a purchaser in times like these. Thomas Carroll knew this, and knew it far too well. He had gone to Baltimore and Washington, and, pocketing his pride, had knocked at every possible door.

It was at this crossroads that Providence intervened. A distant relative returned to Maryland from somewhere in South America; he was not exactly loaded with Inca gold, but he had grown somewhat rich with trade, and he did offer to buy Kingston Hall. With the property he would purchase at least half of the slaves and treat them well, or so he promised. While this distant cousin drove a hard bargain, he had principles and could be trusted. The black folks would not go down the river nor to the cotton fields.

While all this seemed a most unhappy choice, the Carrolls had no other. They must obviously leave great Kingston Hall forever, but they could perhaps buy a smaller plantation and take with them there the best-loved among their household servants. Families need not be broken up, nor would all the field hands be lost. The solution seemed to be expedient and merciful.

Some distance up the Bay, along the winding Choptank River, Thomas and Juliana Carroll came upon a place known as Warwick Fort Manor. The plainish red-brick residence was not too impressive—not after the grandeur of Kingston Hall. It was a considerable comedown in the world. Yet it would somehow hold all of them, and the smaller acreage would at least provide them with food. Thomas Carroll's debts had cut them all down to a very narrow margin, despite the sale of the Hall. The Carrolls were grateful for this haven.

Anne and her sisters (and perhaps even the small brothers too) declared that they preferred the new place, the wider staircase here, and the girls spread their petticoats as proud as peacocks. (Which of course is silly; it is the peacock who is proud, and the peahen who follows after!) But not so with our Anne. They suddenly found, these Carroll girls, a host of new beaux from the countryside around. And the sisters, often engaging in nonsense to cheer up their depressed parents, cried only alone and in secret and in the dark corners of the night, for past, lost glories.

Once the Carroll family felt somewhat settled, Anne felt free enough to make an announcement. She was going off to Baltimore to make her own living, and further, to send some money home. How she would do all this was a question she had not really asked herself, or answered. Still, she had the germ of an idea, and with the spirit and strength of her early twenties she was determined to ride forth like a plumed knight and strive to conquer dragons. How long ago had been those light and carefree days of tournaments in Annapolis, when she had felt herself to be a fragile flower that might perish in the noonday sun.

Leah would of course come along with her. Anne could not see herself ever really separated from Leah. Dearer to her in any real sense than any of her natural sisters was this slim, handsome, understanding black girl. Leah was, in a sense, Anne's alter ego. She was an expert seamstress and could always easily find work. At least, this was what Anne told her naturally anxious parents. As for herself, she was beginning to learn how to look mysterious. With a toss of her flaming locks, that probably fooled nobody, she told them not to worry.

Off on her great personal adventure, with dear Leah beside her, Anne stood firm on the deck of the trim white twin wheeler. Perhaps at the moment she was a little inclined to wish for a round-trip ticket! Anne knew little of big cities, except for her brief experiences in small Annapolis; and Baltimore was then second in size only to New York. As the steamboat raced alongside a rival vessel, whistles split the air; home was behind her, far back across the Bay, and that was where she really felt she belonged.

How noisy the great cities were! Anne could see little of metropolitan glories here along the dingy waterfront, where porters were diligently banging her and Leah's trunks as if determined to destroy them utterly. Ragged urchins thrust newspapers at them, and fishmongers cried their smelly wares above the tumult. Heavy carts rattled along the cobbled streets; and gangs of Negroes, their backs gleaming with sweat, unloaded the heavy cargoes of deep-sea vessels to a deep and monotonous chant: "Lemme go home—I feel so bad I wanta go home!"

As their carriage wound its way through the narrow, crowded streets, past the wide-open taverns where sailors and roustabouts caroused, and past the wheezy laboring of iron winches lifting cargo—bundles and bags that smelled of coffee and spice—Anne was both excited and afraid. She clasped dear Leah's hand, to stop either's trembling. Anne was still only a young girl, determined to become a woman all at once. At this period, and perhaps sometimes later too, she asked a great deal of herself. She was relieved when finally they came into the more respectable sections, the old streets lined with rows of red-brick houses all alike, with white marble stoops and polished railings. These seemed to her to be the real Baltimore.

And yet how could anybody tell which house was his, except by the number on the door? What a queer way to live, Anne thought, nostalgically remembering plantation days.

She leaned out of the carriage for a better look at the fashionable shops on North Charles Street. Scarcely a ship came from Europe that was not stocked with the finest silks, satins, and millinery from Paris. And she knew that ladies from all over the South came here to purchase their wardrobes. Hard by were the jewelers and the silversmiths; it was to Anne a truly magnificent array. "Look there—and there!" Leah, coming out of her first nervous fright, was now becoming as excited as her mistress.

They were now seeing a wonder of the age, a splendid building seven stories high! "Isn't anybody in the world who don't know about Barnum's City Hotel," said the driver proudly, as if he owned it. They would soon be sinking ankle-deep into the carpets from Persia, and viewing themselves in the gorgeous mirrors that stretched from floor to ceiling and back again.

With her eager young face, and her hair glowing bright even against the dingy old upholstery of the hired carriage, Anne was perhaps even enhanced by the presence of her faithful, loving attendant. Leah was the granddaughter of African queens, and showed it. Each of these young women was burgeoning with her own kind of beauty and of youth, and passing gallants whistled and made remarks. It was a little unusual to see such toothsome, attractive specimens of womanhood alone in the streets in a shabby, hired vehicle.

Anne was no doubt glad indeed to escape, at least momentarily, from the stares of the gallants—into the gentility of a boardinghouse, which had been recommended to her father by some authority as "correct." Since Anne was determined to be on her own, Thomas Carroll and his Juliana were wisely letting her try it, naturally with a few parental recommendations. Anne also had the names of many, many friends of the family, of relatives of the Carrolls and the Kings, in her reticule; perhaps she would call on some of them later. But now she had a deep desire to be upon her own!

We can—from this perspective—only imagine the hour when Anne fell across the bed, with her stays unloosed, while Leah sympathetically washed her face with lemon verbena. Anne was now trying, without any immediate success, to still the countless, confusing thoughts that whirled through her pretty and acute head. However, really what could she, even as Thomas Carroll's beautiful daughter, find to do—to *really* do—in Baltimore, where there were, for her at least, no familiar, friendly lanes? And the houses all looked exceedingly like!

These problems could not be solved easily or tonight,

nor immediately in the days to follow. The boldness, so easy to achieve in her girlish dreams, was now receding against hard pressures of reality; the actual realities of a young, booming city, a pressing city full of people who knew their way around, or seemed to at least. And whoever in the world had ever heard of a young woman of gentle birth making her own living as anything but perhaps a poorly paid governess, a teacher, or a seamstress? Up in the North, girls were working in the textile mills, but that seemed the full extent of opportunity for women, of whatever class or background.

Longing to dare and do, Anne pondered her course. If she were a man, she could readily enter some law office and study and qualify. She was actually already widely read in the law, and was better equipped to enter into actual practice than many young men who had already had the temerity to hang out their shingles. Anne's mind, as always, was bouncing, but she was confined still by the arbitrary restrictions placed on her sex, the "dead hand of the past," as Spencer said.

Anne liked being a woman, and she adored the gallant attentions she was always receiving; yet she was not prepared to seek this easy way out. At least she could not follow the format of the other pretty Baltimore belles; the early marriage, the social patterns, the many children, the gracious movements into the past, economically and socially. Anne could not accept this, not until she should meet a man to whom she could give her whole heart! To one of her ardent temperament, it was all—or nothing.

Anne's family needed her financial help, and in this sort of interim period she was determined to assist. Once she took the step, once she married, she would, according to the laws of the time, be classified as an inferior being. Anne, trained in the legalities of the period, was already keenly aware of the potentials. Only a very few exceptional, understanding men, such as her father, could even bring themselves to admit that the fair sex had brains.

Now, however, she must use them! Anne had heard far too much of liabilities and responsibilities in the past years; now she was trying to think of positive things, of assets. She had a busy pen, an always-ready pen, long used to assist her father in the writing of political pamphlets, composing articles for the newspapers, and planning magazine articles to further his projects. From Thomas Carroll she had learned a great deal about how certain political strings could be pulled. Most important of all, the Carroll name was a talisman that could open many doors for Anne and enable her to move in the highest echelons of Baltimore society and business and politics.

Slowly but steadily, Anne began to feel her way into a career that was, at the time, unnamed. It was unheard-of, at the time—this strange, new profession of publicity, and all these contacts and counsels that would sometime come to be known as public relations.

Her own personal charm and her social graces could perhaps be combined with the sharp incisiveness of her mind to further her growing ambitions. She would, if she could, blend the belle with the businesswoman.

8

Glimpses into the Beyond

No one really understood what Anne was about in those days in Baltimore, and perhaps least of all the other people at the house. They raised their eyebrows, no doubt, over her comings and goings on the horse cars. Some were young married couples, who were only stopping here as a sort of step between the honeymoon and the eventual home of their own. Some were old folks gossiping in the parlors, with nothing much to talk about but the past or their present ailments. There were spinsters hoping, and bachelors deferring. The boarding house in early America was an institution, with definite categories, into none of which Anne fitted.

Recent blushing brides, glancing up over their embroidery hoops, envied her. Anne seemed so free, so sure of herself, so meticulously dressed. None of these ladies could know how it really was with Anne, this glamour-girl whom many of them envied. They could not know how sorely the Carroll family needed the few silver dollars that she was sending home from her own maiden ventures into the workaday world and from dear Leah's earnings in a Baltimore mantua-maker's shop.

The fashionable clothes the brides admired were, as often as not, given the new season's twist by Leah's clever fingers. The mantuamaker was a fashion arbiter for a wealthy and somewhat discerning clientele, one which demanded the very latest (whatever it was) from Paris or from London.

Leah worked in a sort of rainbow of silks and satins, and in a flurry of fashion plates that could be later quietly copied at home for her mistress—from the remnants of materials, if need be. Always alert to gossip among the ladies at their fittings, Leah also brought to her mistress word of new shops and business enterprises from which the talented Anne could sometimes pick up a small fee by writing clever letters to selected mailing lists, and doing publicity puffs for the newspapers. She also wrote the small, flamboyant notices that made up the advertising of the period. Anne was pioneering in a new field, one that as time went on would give employment to many thousands of career girls. Her office was largely in her bonnet, and her brief case was a reticule.

But it was all grist to her mill—the fanfare over the arrival of a clipper ship from China with rare oolong teas fit for an emperor, or over the latest appearance of Junius Brutus Booth, the celebrated tragedian and a great Baltimore favorite, accounted the leading Thespian of his time. The baby brought on stage, when the play required it, was dark-eyed little John Wilkes Booth, younger son of the great Junius, who was himself destined to grow up to be a matinee idol over whom the ladies swooned. He was also to take a pistol one night into Ford's Theater in Washington, and with it write the bloody lines of one of the nation's greatest tragedies, the cruel and useless assassination of Abraham Lincoln.

Anne was now well off on her own course, rubbing shoulders with tradesmen and actors, a shocking departure from the prescribed behavior pattern for a young gentlewoman. She was soon, in certain circles at least, almost ranking with the weather as a favorite topic of tea-table conversation. This astounding Carroll girl!

Which was something, because all Baltimorians were (and many still are) deeply versed and interested in their city's changeable and unpredictable weather. They boasted that their hailstones were bigger, their storms more ferocious, their summer heat more stifling than anywhere else; and they sometimes dramatized their two-inch snowfalls by calling them "blizzards" and keeping the children home from school. They had a way of affirming that no one, at any season of the year, should venture forth unequipped with jacket and umbrella, and they often tried to top one another in the use of descriptive adjectives. The citizen who called a day "dank and miserable," was rivaled by someone else who termed it "unspeakably damp and filthy," or by the less imaginative "just horrible."

As for Anne, words sometimes failed even her, though she was less interested in the weather than in the changing climate of the country. It was a time of ferment. Charles Carroll's influence had made the city of Baltimore a center for the infant railroads that now, in spite of the recent financial panic, were growing and extending by leaps and bounds into strapping adolescence.

Even to the end of his long, useful life, Carroll was a brilliant and driving force. Now, in the several luxurious homes his wealth and acumen had provided for his many descendants, Anne was a guest who came and went with the proverbial ease of kinfolk. These were places where young, ambitious men gathered, the future railroad magnates, the entrepreneurs, the drivers. These were the men who were rapidly divorcing Baltimore from the easygoing

South of tradition and making it into a modern metropolis.

Anne was also modern, in the sense that she knew now that she must make her own way with her own talents and her own strengths. She had more than mere beauty; she sparkled with an intelligence and an understanding that made her magnetic; and she found out how to catch the attention of men who could recognize and use her counsel. Also, she had learned how to use men, period.

Her early training in Annapolis had made her adroit. Subtly seeming to invite masculine attentions, she could, at the psychological moment, turn the conversation into other channels. Luscious and lovely, Anne was on her way; she was outgrowing the realms of the little shops and the small tradesmen and moving into the world of high finance and of politics.

Public acceptance (and public investment) in the new railroads must necessarily be solidified before there could be the laying of the ties and tracks that must shimmer into the future, to tunnel through the mountains and swing across the plains and bind the nation together. Public opinion must be guided and shaped to accept the new era— through pamphlets, articles, and other more subtle forms of persuasion. Lavish dinner parties, with lists of important guests carefully screened and seated according to etiquette and protocol could sometimes sway the course of legislatures. Anne, with her feminine intuition and her increasing know-how, could be extraordinarily useful to the rail magnates, and they to her.

In a city like Baltimore, famous for its beauties and for the glitter of its social life, Anne was a unique figure; she was a phenomenon little understood and much talked about. Appearing in public now on the arm of this important man and now again with another, she behaved with a freedom that in anyone but a Carroll would have been deemed scandalous.

Outwardly frivolous and gay, Anne often sought private sanctuary in the book-lined study of the Reverend Robert Jefferson Breckinridge, pastor of the Second Presbyterian Church in Baltimore, and an old friend of her father's. She worshiped at the church with regularity, and from the minister gained the guidance to sustain her through the increasing mazes of her life in Baltimore—and perhaps some of the spiritual and personal balance she felt she required. She was very devoted to this wise and eloquent Kentuckian —as she was soon to be devoted to and adore Henry Clay.

Her own father had now left the embattled ranks of the Jacksonians to rejoin the Whigs, gathered at the moment in convention right there in Baltimore. Introduced formally to Mr. Clay, and with her little hand clasped in his long, nervous fingers, Anne felt a sort of electricity, a personal attention. The great Whig leader had a certain knack for this sort of thing; with the mild flattery he was inclined to extend to any attractive young woman, he asked her opinion about the coming election. Did the Whigs have a real chance?

Obviously Mr. Clay expected only a fluttering, feminine generality from her, but he did not get it. "I'm not so sure," Anne answered slowly and thoughtfully. "I've been hearing about the organized powers working against you. They are strong. They are also underhanded. And they are getting the immigrants naturalized about as soon as the people get out of steerage. Ready to drive them to the voting polls like a flock of sheep, with instructions in their hands. But of course, Mr. Clay, you know all this—" Anne finished, flushing.

In her youthful eagerness to express her indignation at

these illegal procedures, Anne had for a moment forgotten that Henry Clay was a great man; he seemed as of now so human, so real. Perhaps, she had been somewhat presumptuous to think that so experienced a politician, so astute a statesman, would care to hear the reactions of an apparent amateur.

"Yes, I do," said Henry Clay. "But how did you discover it? Women do not usually bother their pretty heads about such heavy matters." His gray eyes were deep and penetrating, and yet somehow they surrounded her with a luminous warmth. "I think I would like to talk more to this daughter of yours," Mr. Clay said to her father, and then went on to invite them to a small, intimate soiree at his hotel the following night. That was to lead to the beginning of many things, at least for Anne.

The convention itself was her first real experience of national politics. Through her father, she had a ringside seat directly beneath the thunderous oratory of Daniel Webster. Webster was quite as she had imagined him; he looked like one of the English country gentlemen she had seen in prints, impressive in his bulk. As he strode about the platform, making his points with flashing eyes and golden tongue, she had the feeling that here was a man who could force other men to believe—but who could not, like Henry Clay, win them. Besides, Daniel Webster was a Yankee, still an alien breed to Anne.

Both men were fiercely ambitious to be President. And both of them had been by-passed for the coveted nomination by William Henry Harrison, the so-called military hero of Tippecanoe, "and Tyler too!" The great gathering, the convention in Baltimore, was in a way a sort of organized protest, taking the spotlight away from the Democrats and rebuilding political fences or building new ones.

During the next busy years Clay, always in the heart of

things, used acuteness, even feminine acuteness, whenever he could find it, to augment his own strength. He had been quick to detect special things in Anne Carroll—understanding to an extraordinary degree. They met at more and more social gatherings, where of course there was more politics going on than simple sociability. These were parlous times, as Anne was beginning to know.

Like many other partisans, young and old, she came under Henry Clay's strange personal spell. It seems that she even fell in love with him. Not romantically, we must hastily add. Clay was sixty-three, and incredibly ancient in her young eager eyes. But she loved the ardor of his spirit and of his acute, incisive mind. Yes, he too was a slaveholder; but he deplored the very institution of slavery almost as deeply as Anne's own father did.

Clay hated too such upstarts as John C. Calhoun, who held purely sectional interests above those of the Union, and who, back in 1832, had seriously threatened to lead a secession group away from it. Mr. Calhoun, Clay observed, used his fine mind but never his heart, if he had a heart at all! But there were many, many like him. Far too many, for the good of the country.

Yet Henry Clay's actions, his life's behavior pattern, were far less violent than his words, many of which words he would only speak in private to trusted friends. He was a man who usually chose the middle way; he was a man of intelligent compromise. It was in his thinking that, if some day both sides gave a little, the really deep issues might be settled or compromised. Both sides, he thought, must give a little, retreat from certain grounds, if the really deep issues were ever to be resolved. Clay was a man of stature and of spirit; he was also a man who could capture the imagination of an impetuous young disciple like Anne, and he had the wisdom and skill to direct it, too. Clay saw the problems of life and of the nation too, in a deeper sense; nothing was all clear—nothing was all black or all white or all anything. Mr. Henry Clay believed firmly in the sensible gray, the so-called middle ground.

Perhaps busy Anne often forgot some of these angles in her work for the coming political campaign. Why could not everyone see, as clearly as she herself did, that Henry Clay was the only possible man who could be the next President of the United States? It was plain as day, to her. He was a deep, thoughtful, patriotic gentleman, and in Anne's mind the nation would be everlastingly lucky to have him at its helm.

But sometimes, in moments of reflection, perhaps she checked herself. If it was true that it was not easy to find an easy solution to her country's life, it was in a way equally difficult for her to find her own paths. But she felt them— and she would find them. They were *there*.

Under the Magnolias

Walking alone underneath the sweet-scented magnolias in the moonlight, Anne longed to give it all up and to abandon herself to romance and domesticity. The feminine side of her heart cried out for that easier way; but her deeper heart, and her deeper mind, could not really accept any man she knew. Her sisters were easier to please. One by one, they were marrying.

If only Anne could really believe in the flowery proposals that came to her now and again! Couched of course in proper Victorian language, they seemed to her as unreal as lines written for an actor to deliver upon a stage. She had her individual dreams, and these did not fancy the Baltimore gallants she had met. She dreamed of a man who could sweep her off her feet. But she had known these Southern gentlemen too long and too well; she had known their families and their histories and had heard about their excessive gambling debts.

Sometime, somewhere, she might find the mate, the man she was seeking. Meanwhile she must amuse herself by being "in love" with somebody—or not. She would enjoy the rosy clouds; but out of them now and then, her despair would not be too deep. She had her work, and she enjoyed it; she really loved living and she flourished like a banner her basic *joie de vivre*. She was also a woman born ahead of her time, and one trying to do too many things all at once. Work could dispel even the pitter-patters of ugly dread; of the creatures of the night that seemed to enlarge into absolutely ghoulish things, haunting her and pressing her.

As the debts at the new, smaller plantation, Warwick Fort Manor, continued to mount sky-high in spite of all the gallant efforts of her father and in spite of what she herself was doing and trying to do, Anne could form a mental picture of the oncoming inevitable—or so it seemed sometimes—conclusion. She could not bear to see any of her dear black friends led in chains across the mountains or sent down the river.

Her younger sisters, as one by one they married, were taking such choice portions of the slaves as they could use and protect. But Anne's brothers were still too young to be of any real assistance. The law of the time was exceptionally cruel. If a man did not pay his debts, his property could be legally attached, and that could mean human property too. Slaves, black friends, members of the family . . .

Anne's brother Tom was studying medicine, and Harry was taking up the law. Perhaps, in the course of time, the boys could, according to their growing, individual abilities, take over, but certainly not yet!

Meanwhile a few of the Carroll's blacks had escaped into the North via the underground railroad. But when they got to New England, to Boston, or even up as far as Canada, what was there for them to do? Freedom yes—but what freedom? The fervent Northern abolitionists who set up and to some extent financed this route to the North must somehow be brought to realize that freedom is indeed an idle promise, if a man has no bread for his belly, no meat cuts for the family stewpot—where was he supposed to go from there and what was he supposed to do?

"If a big beautiful black girl got no home . . ." Anna Ella Carroll was most concerned about these younger slaves, the sturdy young men and the lovely, physically attractive young women. These were the ones who would first attract the eyes of the slave traders. As Anne considered the problem in its entirety, an idea came to her. She herself would somehow buy these slaves from her father. If registered in her name, they could not ever be taken to pay her father's debts—if the foreclosure came.

Anne was contributing regularly to the Carroll family income. Now perhaps they could repay her—with legal deeds to slaves at a nominal $400 each, which was certainly a minimal price. They would then remain upon the plantation, but Anne herself would be the legal owner. It was an ingenious solution with a serious catch to it. Should the plantation be entirely lost, as seemed possible, Anne herself would be held personally responsible for the board and keep of these slaves, these friends, these human beings. It was a most daring step for a young woman not yet thirty and still living only by her wits to undertake.

She could not afford to fail either these or her family. Now, too, Anne was working feverishly in the cause of Henry Clay. He finally had been nominated for the Presidency, and, like many another ardent young idealist throughout the land, she felt that the nation needed him at the helm.

In Illinois, an obscure, gawky thirty-five-year-old country lawyer named Linnkin or Lincoln, or something like that, was an equally dedicated Whig. The ship of state was in a serious difficulty, beset by great and increasing storms.

It required a great statesman to pilot it through these troubled waters.

Antislavery agitation was increasing, what with the furious debates over the proposed annexation of Texas; and war with our southern neighbor, Mexico, loomed in the offing.

As the first results of the election came in, Anne was sure that her man had won. Then it began to appear that James K. Polk of Tennessee was gaining ground, and the wait for final conclusive results was agony for Anne. Counting the votes back in those days was an agonizing and also a tedious process. Communications were slow, and soon the election—which had at first seemed such a quick and easy victory for Clay—started to slip away from him.

"Fraud at the polls!" cried the embattled Whigs, and with reason. In Baltimore alone hundreds of quick naturalization papers had been issued to immigrants on the very eve of the election, and folks had been proved to have sold outright the identity papers of the dead to be used by the living and the unqualified.

Daniel Webster, addressing a crowd in Boston, stated forthrightly that many foreigners who had been in the country less than a month, and who were as ignorant of American ways as they were of its language, had been transformed into voters and used by the unscrupulous opposition as tools. Whisky had bought other votes; ballot boxes had been stuffed so outrageously that some areas handed in a count that well exceeded the total number of adult males.

Fraud had certainly been flagrant; it walked boldly in the streets, and yet it had barely swung the election. Of two and a half million votes cast Clay lost by less than 40,000!

Anne, exercising a woman's privilege, wept unashamedly at the bitterness of life. Why could not the highest honor in the land come to the man who so richly deserved it? The question was one that, in another form, she was to ask of herself years later.

10

Washington Belle

As her public relations work for the newcoming railroads claimed more and more of her time, Anne somehow found herself moving in closer, more and more, to this odd mixture of politics and business. Indeed, at the time the two were becoming so basically interlocked that any thinking person like Anne had to face the fact that each of these economic facets of society was becoming so deeply entwined with the other that they were almost interdependent.

Anne at that time, in her eager way, was sharing the dreams of a whole continent, a growing new world to be someday held together by the span of the shining, silvery lines that would lead across the prairies and through the mountains and which might really weld it into one nation, indivisible.

As she prepared what in our time would be called publicity releases, or press blurbs—and which at the time were only considered pamphlets or letters to the editor—she could also perhaps laugh now at the memory of her own childish, girlish thrills on the great occasion when the first railroad train went out of Baltimore.

There had been a great fanfare, and Anne being Anne,

had hung onto every detail of it all, as told to her by her father. There had been the great parade through the streets of Baltimore. There had been her relative, old Charles Carroll, in his elegant carriage, preceded by dancing youths dressed "as Mercuries, with wings on their feet"; and the procession was augmented by marching bands from the various trade guilds, blowing their heads out and their hearts out—heavy on the brass, as critical musicians would say. But those were the days. Those were Anne's days, as the record shows.

In that first trip of the Baltimore and Ohio Railroad, they ran on wooden rails a distance of little more than twelve miles. The "locomotive" had been a horse or maybe a team of horses.

But soon they would experiment with steam power and would come into competition with Mr. Peter Cooper's little "Tom Thumb," no match for the horse that was placed to race against it. Still, automation had moved in. Men and horses cannot compete with stronger powers: human muscles and equine muscles can do so much and no more.

Now, in Anna Ella Carroll's short span of years, the Baltimore and Ohio had become a power, as had the other new railroads, because of the tying together of a burgeoning nation, the seemingly limitless possibilities of high-speed, economical transportation; so that the crops grown in the new, unfolding West could reach the hungry markets of the East. Surely, Anne thought, wonders would never cease! Samuel Morse had just recently invented the telegraph, and the first line had been installed—all the way from Baltimore to Washington! How strange it all was! Imagine messages actually traveling over wires. Perhaps in some future day people would be even able to communicate, to talk with each other, from far-distant cities. It was a notion almost too extravagant and radical to contemplate; even the first telegraph alone was so startling that people were making fun of it and implying that it was just a parlor magician, pulling a rabbit out of a hat.

Yet Anne, sharp as a tack, had heard some of her railroad associates say that the telegraph could be perhaps very useful to them; they might even adopt this new method of instant communication someday. "What hath God wrought!" This was the first message sent by Morse; it was symbolic of the dawn of a new era. And it was all enough to make Anne feel historic, at the age of twenty-nine!

The railroads were paying her very well for her public relations and publicity services; and any increase of currency in her pocketbook would enable her to buy freedom for another slave, who could then perhaps go forth and be treated with his rights as a human being. But while Anne might be altruistic in her motives, the railroad magnates were certainly not. Fortunes were to be made, and some were then being made through stock and bond manipulations and through the grant of public lands. As everybody knew, minor politicians could be bought any day, a dime for a dozen. But the major figures in the scene must be won over by less simple and obvious means, and through a coercion so tactful that the victims were almost unaware of its very existence.

Anne had been practicing some of these devious arts down in Baltimore, but now the Big Time beckoned. She must transfer herself to Washington. Among her many sponsors and gallants, Anne had a close friend and associate in R. J. Walker, a dry whisk of a man with a personality stripped right down to the bone. He happened to be the political boss of Mississippi, and he had one real interest in life: the pursuit of wealth and the power that goes with it. Already immensely rich, he was at the time backing a new railroad through his part of the South that he thought someday might possibly even extend to the far Pacific.

Anne, with her inner fire and her drive and her public-relations know-how, could be of exceptional assistance even to this cold and calculating man, and well he knew it. Somewhat like the new railroads, most of them still with their vast, extending plans on paper only, the capital city of Washington was in a way just a dream of what the future might bring. But it was still a platform, a stage, for Anna Ella Carroll. She must use it, somehow, someway.

As the celebrated English author Charles Dickens had pointed out during his recent tour of the American provinces, the city of Washington was still just "a city of magnificent intentions." Only by taking an eagle's-eye view of it all, from overhead the still unfinished Capitol, could anyone really comprehend the magnificent designs that were in the hearts and minds of the builders and architects!

But at the moment the city of Washington was in a foul-up: spacious avenues began in a sea of mud and led nowhere. Streets miles long waited hopefully for houses and inhabitants, for public buildings—and for a public. In the wide-open empty spaces, a person like Anne could easily fancy now and then that the season was over, and that the dwellings-to-be had left town with their masters and mistresses.

Perhaps really the most unconcerned among the populace were the swine who served as garbage collectors, and who in this cheerful but unofficial capacity grunted in the courtyards of the best hotels and even accompanied the carriages and coaches to and from shops and restaurants. There were pigs all over! The Whigs humorously gave them the names of leading Democrats, who acidly returned the compliment as soon as possible.

Once Anne was ensconced (with dear faithful Leah) in

a boarding house on Pennsylvania Avenue that served as a jumping-off place for Congressmen, Senators, and other prominent politicians, mostly Whigs, she suddenly found many new doors opened to her in Washington. Through her father and other family connections, she already knew most of the members of the Maryland and of the Virginia bar; the then-powerful Seaton family which ran and published *The National Intelligencer;* Winfield Scott, Chief of Staff of the army; and many other influential personages. A branch of the Carroll family was among the richest in all Washington. Ties of blood and friendship eased Anne's way into a half-built but surging city where a beautiful and respectable young woman, living on her own, was so rare that certainly, without her name and her social entrée, she would probably have had to meet the vilest of suspicions.

Women at best were somewhat scarce in the Washington of that day; at worst, they ran notorious establishments where lonely politicos found solace and comfort—of a dubious sort, indeed. By and large, Washington was a city of men, a city for men. Their families had been left at home, because living was expensive here, housing difficult; and also, as in the case of Juliana Carroll, sometimes wives must remain behind to keep a thoughtful eye on the thousand and one business and intermingled human-business, relationships of the plantation. Or the ancestral homestead— or whatever!

If Anna Ella Carroll had been seeking easy conquests, she could undoubtedly have had men falling into her lap, like ripe apples from the tree. But this was not Anne's way. She sought the difficult, perhaps sometimes the unattainable. She was drawn to men of stature, such as John Minor Botts of Virginia, a man black-haired, blue-eyed, thunderous, a man who always argued furiously with her; they agreed upon practically nothing. They fenced verbally as though to keep the necessary distance between them: they dared not come too close. Drawn by a mutual attraction, they must still deny it: Botts already had a wife.

Emotionally, Anne was far safer serving as hostess for such a man as Senator Tom Corwin of Ohio, who was of her father's age. A temporary bachelor, Corwin was one of the quickest and wittiest men in Washington, and his special personality drew dozens to his hearth. In this semi-Bohemian world of so many men without women—men who gambled, drank their whisky straight, and littered their rooms with cigar ashes, a lovely and intelligent woman like Anne added the missing touch of femininity and gracious formality that cleared the air of dust and smoke. Political debates ranged behind such closed doors as these, with often a frankness and an honesty that illuminated the facets of many issues, facets never disclosed in the halls or on the floors of Congress.

Slowly but surely she was grasping from these Ohioans and others from "up Nawth" a more national point of view, including the North. It all tended to broaden the point of view of this Southern belle: she was seeing things with a new scope.

And some of what she saw frightened her. Even in 1845, the grim outlines of the catastrophe to come were apparent to such men as Henry Clay. Often a guest at his soirees, his Whig gatherings in his suite at the National Hotel, Anne began to share his deep concern over the annexation of Texas. It was to be admitted to the Union as a slave state— but how long could the Union endure with such friction between its individual parts as the recent controversies had revealed? The free states were drawing up in firm opposition to the institution of slavery; and public opinion, which had long been somewhat formless, was beginning to take shape, perhaps alarming shapes. All this could, as Anne was beginning to see, lead to conflicts far more serious than war with then feeble Mexico over the borders of Texas.

The Whigs were a gregarious, stimulating crowd, but Anne did not spend all her time in their circles. As a protégé of R. J. Walker, now Secretary of the Treasury, it was part of her business to associate also with Democrats and thus find out what both sides were thinking.

James Buchanan was often her escort to these Democratic parties and balls; Anne accepted him only as a sort of convenience. To her, even though he was then Secretary of State and now talked about as a possible future President, he was the epitome of the two-faced man who sold his soul to the Devil at the very gates of the church. Anne could place little or no trust in a statesman who had sold out the country for his own personal gain. He had been proved, as much as any individual could be proved, responsible for the shocking election frauds that had led to Henry Clay's defeat in the Presidential election.

Still, Mr. Buchanan clung to her like a leech. Further, to add to her dismay, she discovered that all top Washington circles were now saying that she was about to marry him! Buchanan was wealthy and successful, and, unlike most of the other politicos Anne had met, was really a bachelor.

Many women were after him; he was an excellent catch. And he was so gallant, so attentive that wily Anne, with a woman's intuition, sensed that just now she must watch herself. Mr. Buchanan was useful to her in a business way, in political ways. And she must, in any way possible, avoid that final showdown, that moment when he might propose, and when she would have to say "No!"

She would gladly sell her services as a publicist, as a skillful lawyer—even though she had not technically qualified and as a woman in those days could not possibly be admitted to the bar—but she was just a social lobbyist. Her affections were not for sale or lease.

Meanwhile, among the Democrats, she was beginning to appreciate the brilliant thrusts and the indomitable personality of Stephen A. Douglas, the "Little Giant" from Illinois. Slightly over five feet in height, he had the massive head and shoulders of a much larger man; he had the drive that was already making him one of the real leaders of the Democratic Party. Douglas had a magnificent voice and a personality that could charm—or crush.

Another male personality whom Anne found interesting was one Jefferson Davis, who was to be called "ambitious as Lucifer, and cold as a lizard." He was a complicated and difficult man with a devious mind and at the time working, as was Anne herself, for the interests of R. J. Walker.

Walker had brought Jeff Davis into Washington from his native Mississippi and had started him on his political career as Congressman—and as a Walker tool. At only thirty-seven, Davis was a man with an icy perfection of manner and with a driving desire to forward his own interests.

He had a young wife about half his age, Varina. Daughter of a Natchez planter, Varina had readily assumed the graces of a Southern belle. But like her husband she still had a certain awe of the older aristocracy of Tidewater country, as typified by Anne. Anne was the real "quality" toward which newer planters or landholders out in the farther West and Southwest aspired desperately; and they recognized that she knew—even if she did not say—the difference.

Jefferson Davis was then among the war-mongers in Washington who were rattling the sabers. They were urging war against Mexico, our southern neighbor, already torn with its own strife. It was said that privately Jeff Davis

73

admitted the war with Mexico could lead to many things, perhaps even to the conquest of other Latin lands, to the unlimited extension of slavery, to possibly almost fabulous extensions farther down the pike—to exploitation and empire. Anne trembled; she shook within her heart at the thought of a nation, or even a world, controlled or even swayed by the twisted personal ambitions of a man such as Jefferson Davis.

Henry Clay had wisely advised against this essentially pointless, needless war. Anne, being close to him, knew something of his inner sadness as he had to watch his beloved son go off to the fight. There were now premonitions of disaster to come, seen perhaps as clearly by Anne as by the great Henry Clay himself. It was a time of trouble, increasing trouble. Clay's son was killed in combat, and the aftermaths of this small war were to bring the whole young, emerging nation close to tragedy.

11

Rumbles of Thunder

Since her impetuous descent upon Washington about a year before, Anne had been a frequent guest at the home of venerated General Winfield Scott. He was still Army Chief of Staff and by far the most able and experienced military man in the nation. Now a tangle of political jealousies held him in the capital city, preventing him from taking actual command in the field. He was pacing the floor with frustration, spluttering at the ineptness of General Zachary Taylor, who was, at least from Scott's point of view, doing everything absolutely wrong.

Winfield Scott was a past master of the arts of war. His published works were supposed to be required reading for young officers, yet all too often they were lightly perused and cast aside. One of Scott's few really serious listeners now was Anne; he took pains to explain to her how and why Taylor's invasion of Mexico by way of Monterey was utter foolishness.

"It doesn't strike straight at the target, at the heart of the country! It all leads nowhere." And then he pointed to the map upon his wall and traced with a firm finger the outlines of the formidable barriers of mountain ranges that divided the Monterey area from Mexico City. "Remember this, my girl, it is usually pure geography that can win a war or lose it. Terrain, and its extensions."

Geography, Anne knew, was there forever: firm and solid as the granite of the ages, or sometimes seemingly as circuitous as the rivers of her childhood. It depended upon where one was sitting—from what vantage point one saw or tried to see.

Always eager for knowledge, Anne could, with this experienced, this excellent teacher, begin to understand some of the strategies of war. She was then absorbing not at all out of small feminine curiosity, but out of a deep eagerness to defend this grand man, this man of stature, this devoted servant—one with rank, one with brilliant ideas and insight, but one who was being left somehow outside.

Anne was now being more and more herself, able to see the deeper patterns, the things behind the things, and she was beginning to form new mental patterns for herself.

Many men of position in politics scoffed at Scott, some of them urged by then President Polk. They called Winfield Scott "Old Fuss and Feathers" because of his insistence on military formality. All this made Anne furious. Scott wasn't old; he was a vigorous sixty. If he seemed fussy, it was only because he was playing by the rules, and because some others were stupid or calculating and wanted to make up some new rules of their own.

And perhaps there was another angle here. President Polk very much did not want Winfield Scott to emerge as the hero of the war. It might swing the balance, or several balances. Having been twice a doughty candidate for the Whig nomination for the highest office, Scott could certainly win it this time, as a victorious general, and sweep the Democrats out of Washington.

Now all six-feet-four and all 300 pounds of Winfield

Scott were bubbling and fuming and about to explode. Finally the floundering, the absolute ineffectiveness of General Taylor became so popularly obvious that the President yielded and put the reins back in the hands of a man who could drive.

Scott took the field with the sureness of an expert, an old pro, and struck Mexico tactically at the port of Vera Cruz. He captured the supposedly impregnable fortress, the gateway to the inner heart, and was soon on the march to Mexico City. Following his strategic movements on the map, Anne was impressed with their logic, their sense, and their effectiveness. They worked out as well in action, these military theories, as they had come up on paper. The battles were so quick and decisive that in one of them Generalissimo Santa Ana lost his wooden leg in precipitate flight! Within a few months' time, Winfield Scott and his forces had claimed and won the victory.

Caught in the turmoil of the period that followed this small and senseless war, Anne struggled to keep her own ideals bright. They had indeed suffered with the political defeat of Henry Clay in the last Presidential race. And now General Zachary Taylor was being called the true, resounding hero of the Mexican war. His minuscule, peripheral victory at Buena Vista was by some so-called authorities being ranked high above the vital capture of Mexico City and Chapultepec, and Taylor was seemingly the man of the hour! To Anne, all this was so blind, so unfair and unjust. Politicians would try to have the public believe that black was white; they would twist the truth into odd forms just to serve their own devices of the moment. Anne was a woman fierce and determined in her devotions: her temper was not a cool one. Things added up or else they didn't; two and two had to make four!

And at the moment Jeff Davis was riding high on the

crest with Zachary Taylor, his former father-in-law. Davis as a young West Point graduate had married Sarah Taylor, who had fallen victim to malaria and died within a few months. Davis was making the very most of the somewhat tenuous relationship he had with Zack Taylor—and proudly displaying the scars of the minor wounds he had received in the engagement; he was also declaring, along with Buchanan, that "destiny beckons us to hold and to civilize Mexico!"

Financially, Anne was now doing better than ever before since she had gone off on her own. But she was still uneasy. Material security did not reassure her, not in the face of the serious questions that the Mexican war had raised. Organized opposition to the extension of slavery into new lands flamed afresh.

When the United States agreed to pay the tottering Mexican government fifteen million dollars for the fair province of California and the far Western territory then called New Mexico, but which even included parts of the later states of Nevada, Utah, Arizona, Colorado, and Wyoming, Jeff Davis and other extremists deplored the transaction. Why pay a penny for these hundreds of thousands of acres when they could have been grabbed, along with Mexico itself? And why stop there? What was to keep slaveholders from extending their domains clear down into Central America?

Davis was a man who would be king, and he was not alone in his thinking. Southerners generally were becoming alarmed at the attitude of the North. Men up there were saying in press and pulpit that the institution of slavery should not be allowed to spread further, not even within the boundaries of our own country. Perhaps the time had come, some radical Southerners felt, for the South to leave the Union altogether and to make its own decisions.

Rumbles of thunder resounded with frightening force in Washington, and re-echoed through the land. Horrified by the violent secessionist ideas expressed so volubly by Jefferson Davis and others of his ilk, Anne still felt convinced that this was not just bravado. Certain documents were coming her way, to which she had access through her work for the Southern railroads, which showed all too clearly that the groundwork for secession was being laid, even to the actual timing of it, and as to which state would be the first to make the break. To men like Henry Clay and Daniel Webster, and to Anne herself, this was the work of traitors.

The Union must be saved, whatever the cost to the ambitions of individual men, in spite of hurt sectional pride and stubbornness that masqueraded as patriotism. In the name of common sense, both sides must yield! Clay was in his seventies now, his spirit broken by the loss of his beloved son, his ambitions to be President gone. The years had taken their toll of his strength, but had left unimpaired his qualities of statesmanship. He was masterly at compromise, and now for the last time he would bring his incomparable art into play to try to strike the chord of unity. "One nation, indivisible," the whole gaining strength from its separate parts, which standing alone would be weak.

The situation was crucial and increasingly delicate, the issues so involved that any one of them could blow up at the slightest jar and burst the nation into bits. Anne, sometimes taking her preferred place in the visitors' gallery of the Senate, felt the electricity of tension and suspense. John C. Calhoun was in a wheel chair. Henry Clay was so exhausted with preparation of argument that she had seen a friend all but carry him up the steep Capitol steps. The fire of Daniel Webster, too, was soon to be extinguished, as the giants of the Senate came to grips and engaged in what was to be their final battle.

Either the aristocratic, chauvinistic South must continue to dominate and have its will prevail, as it had for most of the seventy-five years of the nation's history, or it would secede. This was Calhoun's grim but sincere conviction; his was a profound dedication to the doctrine of States' rights. Too weak sometimes to read his own words as the days passed, Calhoun sat swathed in flannels there in the Senate, his great deep eyes flashing as a friend read from manuscript the speeches of this powerful and distinguished champion of nullification and the institution of Negro slavery. Tossing the gray mane of his hair, Calhoun was taunting the North, demanding the impossible; he was doing his utmost to provoke a break. With the canny instincts of a veteran politician, he realized that this was the time, if ever, for the South to strike out. It was still strong by comparison with the North, but the years were coming when it might be overwhelmed.

More than once during these debates, Anna Ella Carroll stormed out of the visitors' gallery, her temper to be calmed only by such feminine distractions as getting her hair done, planning a ravishing new sapphire-blue silk dress with a sweeping train for her next theater date with a new beau, and a determination to be frivolous for an entire evening without a word about politics.

But she could not stay long away from the Senate, not at this time. Too much was bubbling; too much was impending. By the time Henry Clay finally took the floor, feelings were so impassioned among the Senators and for that matter throughout the country at large, that chances for civil war were evident and increasing. No one, not even the great Mr. Clay, could bridge the gap with compromise. Every point he proposed provoked further animosity, further schism. California should be admitted to the Union as a "free" state. "Never!" cried the Southern bloc. The South insisted on a drastic law for the return of fugitive slaves. "Not while we can defeat it!" Northern gorge had risen.

Anne and the others in the Senate gallery were watching one of the greatest dramas of history, or at least in the history of the United States. The scenery of subterfuge and concealment had all been shoved aside, and the chief actors were performing with the bare bones of their beliefs exposed. Like many anxious newspaper readers North and South, the audience had a sense of personal participation; what was being determined here might be their own future, their own individual destiny.

Henry Clay, a Kentuckian and a slaveholder, was said to be making concessions to the North, and thus making himself a traitor to his own section. Answering the bitter gibes, Clay's voice rang out with his devotion to the nation, which was equally as strong as Daniel Webster's. Clay said, "I have heard something said about allegiance to the South. I know no South, no North, no East, no West, to which I owe any allegiance!"

His oration, moving and inspiring almost beyond mortal ken, lasted for two days. It was almost as though his aged strength was being sustained by some miraculous, higher power. When at last he finished, a great hush fell over the crowd gathered within and without the chamber. And then suddenly they stormed him, men and women alike hysterical with adulation. Anne had never so loved old Henry Clay, nor had she been so completely swept into the cause for which he was devoting the last full measure of his life.

It was only a brief interlude before Clay's plea for union and for compromise was torn to bits by angry men. And as the days and weeks of that bitter spring passed into the summer of 1850, minor figures came and went, trying to get into the act, as they say in show business. Journalists scribbled their pencils to the nubs, and the ears and minds of the public were choked with verbiage, mostly sound and fury signifying nothing. Of all or most of this, Anne was an interested, a fascinated, and an increasingly devoted and thoughtful observer.

In the midst of the rising tumult, Daniel Webster sat grimly silent, listening to the contestants, weighing his doubts. When he at last arose to give what perhaps was his greatest or at least most extraordinary oration, it was with the air of a man fully aware that his weight could determine the outcome. Speaking with a mighty eloquence, he also, like Clay, disclaimed all sectionalism. "I wish to speak not as a Massachusetts man, nor as a Northern man, but as an American. Hear me for my cause!"

Any other course but compromise was ruin for the nation, he said. And then with magnificent courage he went on to disappoint the fervent Northern abolitionists by not expressly excluding slavery from the new Western territories and by supporting in part the South's demands for a forcible Fugitive Slave law.

After a checkered lifetime, marked with roaring ambition and self-seeking plans, the golden-voiced Mr. Webster destroyed himself politically with this speech, but in the minds of many at last reached noble stature.

With the final passing of the Great Compromise of 1850, the ominous rumbles of thunder receded to mutterings. By heroic and costly personal sacrifice, Henry Clay and Daniel Webster had averted the dread day of decision, or so it seemed.

12

Lightning Forks
the Sky

Tensions relaxed, and again the capital city of Washington returned to its social merry-go-round. With highborn Southern women keeping a firm hold on the reins, society there was frequently termed the main business of life. Upstarts and newcomers found it practically impossible to work their way into the gilded circles where Anne had been received as part of her birthright and where she was now becoming famous as a hostess.

It was no secret that the more lavish of the Washington affairs were given to promote political and commercial interests and paid for accordingly behind the potted palms. Most of Anne's parties were no exception to this rule, and yet she still had a definitive edge. Hers was a unique combination of beauty with brains, of Southern aristocrat with efficient businesswoman. Thus, her major parties gave a social cachet to those invited, and her guest list was a roster of who-was-who at the moment in Washington.

Satin trains swept up the steps of exclusive hotels, entering from polished broughams. Gentlemen praised the superb cuisine and the choice of wines. Diamonds glittered on bosoms that were none of them more curvaceous than

Anne's, as, making graceful introductions and smoothing the way for important contacts, she made her parties bubble like the glasses of champagne which flowed so freely.

It was inevitable that many women were jealous of her and her freedoms. Among them were her several sisters. Reading the society columns in the quiet circumspection of their Tidewater homes, they preferred to forget that it was only Anne, among all the Carroll girls, who had dared to brave the outside world and try to do something to save the failing family fortunes: they criticized her endlessly. She was, in their eyes, much too bold, much too much in the public eye, too adventurous in her romances, real or imagined by them.

Women seeking grounds for criticism found it readily. Among these was Mary Todd Lincoln, who though not personally acquainted with Anne, resented the snubs of the entire Washington social system which had fallen into such rigid forms of caste. A former Kentucky belle of status, Mrs. Lincoln had hoped to promote herself and her husband socially in Washington but had found herself ignored. Moping in a dreary boardinghouse, she brooded and fumed. They couldn't do this to her! Though the system was nothing of Anne's devising, she would someday be made to suffer for it.

Incandescent as the sought-after Miss Carroll might appear in public, she had sometimes a wistfulness in private. It was a quality that a fashionable portrait painter for whom Anne sat had the perception to catch. Her coloring was splendid on canvas, hair deepening now to an auburn that mingled with Titian red and burnt sienna and the umber of a painter's palette to frame an ivory-white complexion. The blue eyes were bright with spirit and intelligence; shoulders and bosom revealed "a fine figure of a woman." It was only the artist's rendering of the mouth that revealed the other side of Anne—appealing, tender, a fervent pursuer of dreams.

Often, wearied by the strenuous times in Washington, she would return to the peaceful, lazy rivers of her childhood and the security her father's presence always gave. Juliana was no longer there except in memories close and dear. Surrounded by law books that managed to smell of wisdom and old leather, Anne for a while forgot the turbulence of the times in which she was living so vividly and the ominous storm warnings of the conflict to come. She threw herself down upon the sweet-scented grass of summer and looked at the happy sailing clouds overhead.

Tidewater country was always the same; it had an all-pervading and ageless charm to which one could easily succumb—but she could not completely forget the acrid debates in Congress on the Compromise of 1850 and the strident fierceness between South and North. It could no longer be tempered by Henry Clay and Daniel Webster. They had dared to transcend party politics, no matter what the personal cost, but lesser men had succeeded them.

Forces beyond the control of any individual were ceaselessly at work to destroy the union of the states. The times were moving inexorably from the agrarian civilization of the eighteenth century, which the South still embodied, into the modern world. Could the transition be made without bloodshed?

Rash heads were prevailing and rash words being spoken, making slavery the excuse that far transcended any other issue. The North was churning with the wheels of industrial progress, run by steam and energy and new ideas. The West was rising with the yeast of a new free America, where any man might swing an ax and clear a farm, read law at night, debate with his neighbors, and by his own efforts rise to prominence. The country was static only in the

South which clung to its traditional ways of life with a growing desperation, the desperation of bewilderment and fear. A proud section would not willingly become a poor relation outvoted by all the new free states—Wisconsin, Iowa, California and others crowding—and furthermore be called a sinner!

The owning of slaves, black slaves, had become an essential way of life in Dixie. In the North, the slaves were white and were called factory help but subjected to toil as grinding as any in the cotton fields. But the economic course of the nation was against black slavery; too many hands for too little work. It would disappear of its own weight, thoughtful men were saying and writing, given time. . . .

Unfortunately, many reformers and abolitionists were impatient at the slow course of social evolution. They saw in slavery an evil that should be destroyed immediately, as one might scourge a visible devil with a tail and cloven hoofs. Both sides quoted from the Bible and from the Constitution; press and pulpit hurled denunciation, and common men took sides.

Harriet Beecher Stowe's *Uncle Tom's Cabin*, with its slanted picture of Simon Legree lashing Uncle Tom, with Eliza crossing the river and leaping from one cake of ice to another with her baby in her arms just ahead of the bloodhounds, did nothing to smooth things over. It was, if ever, a time that called for sanity and sense; for the cool quiet voice of reason. Raised still by some men, it was a voice seldom heard above the thunder of the approaching storm. . . .

Going about her business in the North and the middle South, Anne smelled the ozone of lightning that streaked the sky above a nation that might not long endure. Daughter of a border state, she could see both points of view, as had her mentor, Henry Clay. Whatever the years ahead might hold for the nation, she had her personal and ever-present involvement with the slavery problem. She was mortgaging her future to solve the immediate segment of it that came within her own control.

Through the earlier arrangement with her father, she had already purchased twenty black girls who had remained on his plantation, eating him out of house and home. Some of the girls were mothers now; black boys were growing into stalwart men, and—as always—the slave traders hovered like vultures. Under the new and rigorous Fugitive Slave Law, none could be permitted to "escape" into the North without the severest of penalties levied against the frail and aging Thomas Carroll.

Anne had planned to free the girls she owned, but now there was no help for it. She must use their market value as collateral to back the notes she was signing to protect the other young folk from being snatched as prizes to cover the debts her father had incurred, and was always incurring, to maintain them. The older slaves, past the age of usefulness in the fields, were not in danger.

Several wealthy abolitionists, among them the noted and always generous Gerrit Smith, came to her aid with money, but a shameful proportion found it convenient merely to wish her well and Godspeed. As Anne went about her quest in Washington and New York, pocketing her pride to plead for other human beings, her thoughts must have been bitter ones. How easy it was for Northern orators to prate of freedom in the abstract where it would cost them nothing! When it came down to the particular, how tight they tied their purse strings!

Through the years, Thomas Carroll had had various political appointments, but they had been of short duration. Her brothers Tom and Harry had given help when they could; but, like the sisters, they were involved with their own lives and left it to Anne to bear the brunt of their common human inheritance.

Anne was clever and strong. She would manage; she always had. She moved in a glamorous world, knew everybody of influence, and made money easily, or so it seemed to them. Tom was now a country doctor, beloved by his patients, but more often than not paid off by them only in hams and sides of beef. Harry was in and out of one business after the other, never successfully. Her sisters, mostly married now, were restricted by their husbands and by the conventions then placed on gentlewomen. They were also burning with sibling jealousies at the obvious preference Thomas Carroll had for his first-born; and, while Anne had overthrown the taboos against a lady's making money, her sisters were not of her mettle.

A woman should be able to stand on her own two feet if need be, Anne had often said, looking down at the dainty slippers that encased two of her most admired beauty points. Seeing her at a party, vibrant and gay, with the erect carriage and the air which always distinguished her, few could suspect the burden that lay across her fashionable shoulders with such deceptive lightness.

As though fate were shifting the scene from the problems in and around Washington which appeared to be insoluble, the discovery of gold in California had precipitated a fevered rush to the West. A new hope and stir were abroad in the land. Wheels of prairie schooners rolled across the Great Plains, despite the threat of hostile Indians, high mountain passes, and trails that often led to death. Sailing vessels headed into the winds for the long and perilous journey around the Horn and up the thousands of stormy Pacific miles that led to California and to the mother lodes of gold.

Enterprising men were hurrying plans for a shorter route by rail or canal through Nicaragua. Now Anne was working for Cornelius K. Garrison, the gentlemanly but astute entrepreneur, in his efforts to best a formidable rival in the person of another Cornelius, the ruthless Vanderbilt. Garrison had been in the steamboat business on the Mississippi and he was a friend of Anne's uncle in St. Louis, but he had come East to speed his operations and to enlist her particular skills. By this time Anne—while of course not permitted to practice—was an extremely competent and experienced railroad attorney.

It was the lure of gold, too, that was giving impetus to the hue and cry for a railway which would span the entire North American continent from Atlantic to Pacific. As forces rallied to fight for government support and public support of a northern or a southern route, Anne's special services and know-how were at a premium.

Professionally, she had grown up with the east coast railroads. Now her expertise in the legal technicalities and in finding a way through the tangled web of personalities and politics that could impede or implement action brought her fees large even for a man, and so extraordinary as to be unheard-of for a mere woman.

Gravitating between New York, Washington, and Baltimore, and between secret conclaves and her littered writing table, Anne was putting her various pamphlets and miscellaneous writings into the form of a book that would be something more than an impressive publicity piece to plead the railroads' cause. *Star of the West* was all of that, of course, but she managed to give it the wider scope of her own national vision. She pointed out that railroads, extending their web of networks, were actually iron bonds holding the Union together—or could be. Communication between the divergent, widely separated parts of an enormous new country; quick transportation of people, freight, foodstuffs and, if need be, of munitions, too, were vital to the wholeness of the nation.

As with the book she had published in the previous year (1856) *The Great American Battle,* Anne posed challenging questions. The book had been a fearless and forthright attack upon the exploitation by unscrupulous politicians of the immigrant vote, as an attempt to distort the American dream of democracy. Anne saw great injustice in using these newcomers, many of whom spoke no English and who knew nothing about the issues involved, until at least they had been somewhat assimilated into the melting pot. The book had sold thousands of copies and had made her name known far outside Washington and her usual circles of influence. She never had any pretensions to great literary genius, but she wrote with a force and flamboyance that attracted and interested widely divergent groups. Anne was a publicist, and she had a knack of being timely, with her slender fingers on the national pulse.

Publicly she enjoyed the trust of many influential men, but her private life was her own affair. All of the letters and notes that came to her were certainly not concerned solely with business. Addressed to "My dear Miss Anne," some glowed with an old-fashioned ardor which their discreet phrasing could not entirely hide, and many of them bore a foreign postmark.

Millard Fillmore, sojourning in Italy, was turning to her as a confidante. She had always been drawn to Fillmore and had come to know him well during the stormy days of debate that had led to the Compromise of 1850. As Vice-president under Zachary Taylor, he had been the presiding officer of the Senate until the summer of that crucial year. With Taylor's death in July, Fillmore had become President and had lent the full force of his office to passage of the bill that had saved the Union, for a time, anyway.

Unlike Buchanan, he was a man she deeply respected and admired. While there were some who might call him a mere politician, she knew well that Fillmore had the courage of conviction. He was not brilliant, like Clay and Webster, but he stood steadfast where lesser men would have quailed and capitulated. He was self-made—no inherited privileges his—and he was wealthy. With her deep sensitivity to emotional as well as to political undercurrents, Anne knew that Fillmore had marriage on his mind. But should she encourage him? The question was a hard one to decide. From every rational point of view, Fillmore would make an excellent choice for a husband. He could give her comfort, companionship, and security. He was still active in politics, and she could share in his ambitions. With Fillmore she would not be going it alone and need not tremble over the menacing lightning flashes and the rumble of thunder—"the thunder on the left" as the ancient Romans called it, which presaged great and terrible events.

Yet if she married him, she would no longer be Anna Ella Carroll; she would just be Mrs. Millard Fillmore. It is possible that her hesitation came from a subconscious reluctance to change her status from that of a free agent to that of a satellite; that she remembered that her mother Juliana had died prematurely from too much childbearing, and that her sisters after marriage had become practically nonentities.

And Anne was a free soul, a woman completely feminine, yet with a man's mind in one sense. She thought for herself.

With Fillmore's return to America, she began to promote him most actively as Presidential candidate for the new American Party formed largely of the respectable elements of the expiring Whig party, but embarrassed by a radical fringe of irresponsible "Know-Nothings," who were riding on the Whig coattails. It was a mix-up of a party, reflecting the ferment of the times, and Anne soon became a target for the more vicious of the partisans. She was interested in Mr. Fillmore, rumor had it, not because he was a man who could again help to preserve the Union but as a prospective husband; she was, they said, promoting herself for the position of First Lady.

Actually Anne was doing all that lay within her feminine power to try to prevent the country's choice of one who could only be a weak President—James Buchanan. A figurehead such as he was could not possibly carry the ship of state through the storms that lay ahead. With Buchanan's election, she must have laughed wryly at those who had been sneering and deriding her efforts. She could well have been Buchanan's lady. Did no one remember earlier tales that had romantically linked their names? Did no one, not even her family, know what kind of person she really was?

Anne could never, never settle for a marriage of convenience, not even with a man she sincerely admired, as she did Millard Fillmore. He did not excite her; he did not overwhelm. And she was not a woman who could let her head rule her innermost heart.

13

The Storm Breaks
on Lincoln

It was enough to make Anne's blood boil—idealism and patriotism marred and smeared with an ugly tarbrush! The "Know-Nothings," jubilant over their alliance with the new American Party, were using it as a cover up for secret machinations. They were groups of men who, when questioned about violent acts against immigrants, retreated behind a cloak of silence. They "knew nothing." They terrorized elections in such centers as Baltimore by organizing themselves into clubs that bore such unattractive names as "Plug-Uglies," "Rip-Raps" and "Blood-Tubs"! The great poet and journalist, Edgar Allan Poe, in the fading incandescence of his genius and his despair, had been one of their earliest victims. Even his premature death has been blamed upon a senseless beating they gave him. At any rate, during this period decent citizens remained indoors at night, fearful of the gangs of toughs that roamed the streets. In fact, Baltimore was earning the unenviable title of "Mob-town"!

Yet the foreign vote was no longer a major issue, as Anne herself was quick to realize. Events were moving so swiftly, precipitated by civil war in Kansas, that another new political party known as "the Republicans" could well be the tinder that would ignite the entire country, like the blast of a prairie fire. The Republican Party had started in a little white schoolhouse in Ripon, Wisconsin, and it was firmly opposed to the further extension of slavery.

Anne, with her intimate connections through the South, was only too sharply aware how little provocation its hotheaded leaders needed to make their long-planned and final break with the Union. She happened to know that a secession party had been formally organized at Jackson, Mississippi, as early as 1849, and that Jeff Davis and his colleagues had already sketched a constitution for a Southern Confederacy, of which Davis, of course, would be president.

Anne's work with R. J. Walker had made available to her much supposedly secret correspondence, such as that which passed in 1850 between Governor Seabrook of South Carolina and Governor Quitman of Mississippi:

Let me, however, reiterate the assurance that South Carolina is prepared to second Mississippi or any other State in any and every effort to arrest the career of a corrupt and despotic majority. She is ready and anxious for an immediate separation from a Union whose aim is the prostration of our political energies. May I hope that Mississippi will begin the patriotic work and allow the Palmetto banner a place in the ranks.

Later, in her historic *Reply to Breckinridge*, she was to make public many such letters that had aroused her attention.

The Great Compromise had been, at best, a patch-up bandage over wounds that continued to fester. Was there a man alive who now could forget sectional interests and emerge with a cure? Plenty of men were eager to try. And Anne, recovering from her deep disappointment over Fillmore's defeat, was well acquainted with the more prominent ones.

Stephen A. Douglas was almost certain of the next Democratic nomination. And Whig factions combining with Free-soil Republicans were talking about running William H. Seward of New York. Anne still had hopes for her old friend John Minor Botts and the American Party, but these were fading.

The national brew was certainly in a stew! Anne, reverting to one of the Tidewater expressions she liked to use, said that everyone was ready to put in the potatoes and onions but none had fetched the rabbit!

As the limelight played on Douglas and Seward, both brilliant national figures of some years' standing, few were watching the gawky, uncouth, relatively obscure Springfield lawyer, Abraham Lincoln. Anne herself had known Lincoln casually when they were both neophyte Whigs in the orbit of eager young workers in Washington that had encircled Henry Clay. Lincoln had made no great splash here, or as a Congressman.

But now, as Anne began to hear his name mentioned again, she recalled that in some ways he resembled Henry Clay. They were both men whose faces, ugly in repose, came alive when they spoke, their features luminous. And each had, in his utterances, the pith and force of the language of the frontier.

Sitting silent, Lincoln had been grotesque, as Anne remembered him. Clothes had hung upon his long, gaunt frame as upon a scarecrow; teacups slipped from his knees, and social persiflage embarrassed him. He was a curious man; one almost might say an oddity. He had not worn a coonskin cap, but Anne could easily imagine him in one!

Yet times had changed. The situation called for strange deeds, possibly only to be performed by strange and unorthodox men. Anne knew little of the prairies and the dust of distant Illinois, and yet a voice was ringing from them, this summer of 1858, striking a note of truth. Lincoln, Republican candidate for Senator, and Douglas, the Democratic nominee, were stomping the state in a series of public debates. Everywhere enormous crowds were gathering to hear them and, encircling the various towns with their campfires, giving the whole the color of some huge carnival or county fair. The strongest man who swung the mallet and rang the bell at the top of the pole was to win the box of cigars. That was the way it was; that was the way they did things out West. Or did all this have far greater significance?

Swinging in a hammock at Castle Haven, the Tidewater home her father now shared with brother Tom and where she was always welcomed with open arms, Anne wondered. Trying to relax from the turmoil of Washington, she was electrified instead. The press was covering the Lincoln-Douglas debates with legions of reporters, and in the Tidewater, as elsewhere throughout the country, there was talk of little else.

Through the columns of the New York papers, Anne was watching the little-known, presumably shambling and inexperienced Mr. Lincoln parry, thrust, and throw "the Little Giant" Douglas on the day's most burning issues. With what clarity the man spoke—and with what knowledge of the Constitution and all that America should stand for!

Accustomed to politicians and their highflying verbiage, their play upon public emotions for their private, immediate purposes, she began to feel that Lincoln might be different. Often the man from Springfield struck a deeper note than any she had heard. And earlier, in the speech with which he had accepted the Republican nomination, he had said:

If we could first know *where* we are, and *whither* we are tending, we could better judge *what* to do, and *how* to do it. . . .

96

'A house divided against itself cannot stand.' I believe this government cannot endure permanently half *slave* and half *free*. I do not expect the Union to be dissolved, I do not expect the house to fall; but I *do* expect it will cease to be divided. It will become *all* one thing, or *all* the other!

These were ringing words. It was a time that called for greatness. Could Lincoln possibly be the man? Abstracted in deep thought, Anne heard the wail of her little niece. The child had brought her a bouquet of field flowers, and Auntie Anne had unwittingly pulled off all the petals. Anne cradled the little girl in her arms as they both rocked in the hammock. How could one explain to a child that sometimes grownups were thinking so hard they didn't realize what their hands were doing?

Anne and her father had many visitors these summer days, but not, as of yore, for purely social reasons. Neighbors and friends were deeply troubled. They wanted to know from Anne what really was going on in Washington, as though she or anyone else could tell them! The great trees that surrounded the ancient mansion and made it an oasis of coolness, and the green lawns that sloped down almost to the bay, were the setting for impromptu debates far less theoretical than those out in Illinois. Here in old Maryland, a border state, folks were talking about the problems of slavery and abolition from the pages of their own lives, and about Union or secession with a personal involvement with which one might discuss continuing a strained marriage or asking for a divorce.

Should civil war actually come, Maryland could go either way. Retreating from the clouds of hungry mosquitoes which swirled over the lawn at night, Anne and her father often sat long in the study with Thomas H. Hicks, who had a small plantation nearby and also ran a line of steamboats. Beneath his mild manner, Hicks was a strong Union man, and she and Thomas Carroll were stirring up his political ambitions to run for governor of the state.

She could do nothing about Lincoln out in Illinois. He had, as most people expected, lost the Senatorial election; and few were yet convinced that he was the man of the hour. He was reputed to be capturing the imagination of the West, but most Easterners were dubious. They much preferred Seward as a Presidential candidate, a man of tried performance as Governor of New York and long its Senator, to an unpredictable individual who had not even been able to carry his own state.

Nevertheless, people were curious about Lincoln and would not dismiss him utterly without an actual hearing. They were to have it in New York City in the early spring of 1860. Lincoln was to speak at Cooper Institute, gathering place of the city's intelligentsia. And Anne was among the scores who hastened up from Washington to attend. Slipping across icy streets and wading through mud and slush, she entered the hall where William Cullen Bryant, literary idol of the East, was already ensconced upon the platform. Beside him was the great editor, Horace Greeley. Indeed, as one reporter remarked, no speaker had faced such a general assemblage of culture and intellect since the days of Clay and Webster.

Anne had forgotten how tall Lincoln was, how his long, bony frame unlimbered with his stride. Swiftly arranging his notes upon the lectern, he faced the crowd with a self-possession that had not been his in earlier years. The unruly shock of black hair, the swarthy complexion, the features carved ruggedly as though by strokes of his own ax—all this she remembered. The years had not polished him much, she thought.

As he began to speak, his mouth lost its ungainliness, his heavy eyes their listlessness; and presently he was clearing cloudy issues with a lucidity of reason and judgment that made a profound impression upon his sophisticated audience:

. . . It is exceedingly desirable that all parts of this great confederacy shall be at peace, and in harmony, one with another. Let us Republicans do our part to have it so. Even though much provoked, let us do nothing through passion and ill temper. Even though the Southern people will not so much as listen to us, let us calmly consider their demands, and yield to them if, in our deliberate view of our duty, we possibly can. . . .

The question recurs, what will satisfy them? Simply this: we must not only let them alone but we must, somehow, convince them that we do let them alone. . . .

Wrong as we think slavery is, we can yet afford to let it alone where it is, because that much is due to the necessity arising from its actual presence in the nation; but can we, while our votes will prevent it, allow it to spread into the national territories, and to overrun us here in these free states? If our sense of duty forbids this, then let us stand by our duty, fearlessly and effectively. . . .

LET US HAVE FAITH THAT RIGHT MAKES MIGHT, AND IN THAT FAITH, LET US, TO THE END, DARE TO DO OUR DUTY AS WE UNDERSTAND IT!

For two hours Abe Lincoln had entranced his listeners; no man ever before had made such an impression on his first appeal to a New York audience. Here was no "Black Republican" carried along upon the extremes of abolition. Lincoln was middle-of-the-road, seeing both sides of the question as Henry Clay had, and as Anne herself was trying to do. Still, she could not believe that Lincoln would ever be elected President.

She would work instead for Stephen A. Douglas, who had proved himself a vote getter. Douglas was a known quantity, and he was opposing ever more forcefully the extension of slavery. As a close-to-professional politico herself, Anne could not afford to back a mysterious X factor, eloquent though he be.

Anne was shocked when the Democratic Party splintered. It had seemed the most whole and cohesive of any of the parties, but it seemed that anything could happen in these hectic days. Southern delegates had bolted rather than accept Douglas, and they named John C. Breckinridge. Breckinridge—what an insolent, opinionated pup he was! Anne's anger knew no bounds. He was the nephew of the pastor whose friendship and advice had meant so much to her during her early days in Baltimore; now he must be breaking the old man's idealistic and loyal heart!

Now, whomever the Republicans nominated was sure to win the election. Seward had everything in his favor, everything in the bag, except that the nominating convention was to be held in Chicago. The West was moving in against the East; and the American Party, still strong in many sectors and in which Anne was still a leader, was conscious of its not inconsiderable remaining weight.

Chicago was determined that Lincoln, the rail splitter, born in a log cabin, the friend of the poor and the pioneer, should be the country's choice. To this end, the young enterprising city on the shores of Lake Michigan had built a huge, ramshackle structure known as the Wigwam for use as a convention hall, a name as laughable to wealthy, influential Easterners as the fact that they must make the long trek out to Illinois. It was all crude and ridiculous.

But the rough, raw city was putting on a great and startling show. As one of the Eastern newspaper correspondents reported to his editor, "I am writing this under every obstacle—a cannon is exploding on the roof!" It was not to be a polite or "fancy" convention; and the effete

Easterners must accept the rough-and-tumble of Western politics, politics in the raw with no holds barred. As for the Southerners, God help them!

The special trains rolled in from the East, decorated with many banners and filled with smug contingents of delegates who looked askance at the boardwalks that raised Chicago only inches above the seemingly bottomless mud. Sneering at hotel accommodations which were certainly on the primitive side (three and four to a room and sometimes as many to a bed), they assured themselves that the convention was a cinch for Seward. A bit too noisily and confidently, perhaps. American Party delegates in other delegations were testing the atmosphere and reporting all reactions by telegraph to Washington. Which way should they swing?

Anne wished that she could be there in Chicago to see it all firsthand, to hear how it was when absolute pandemonium broke loose with the introduction of the name of Abraham Lincoln. Up until then Seward's nomination had been greeted politely, if calmly, as an accomplished fact. For Lincoln, however, the galleries had been packed, and roared their preference, so the reporters wrote, hastily filing their releases. From smoke-filled rooms in Chicago, the telegrams sped to smoke-filled rooms in Washington, where Anne and others of the American Party had assembled in a council of war. The word came in: First ballot: Seward 173½ votes, Lincoln 102. Needed to nominate: 233 votes.

In the tension-packed period of the minutes between telegrams, Anne said that she had decided she favored Lincoln and would work for him. She said it quietly, so as not to sway the others. This was a vital decision each individual must make for himself. But others nodded and fell in with this beautiful, brilliant, influential, Titian-haired woman. It was soon settled. The American Party would join other still powerful factions and go all out for Abraham Lincoln.

Third ballot: Lincoln 231½ votes. Needed to nominate: 233. The Ohio delegation by instruction shifted its vote, and Abe Lincoln, the rail splitter, was the nominee!

At the announcement of the vote, men leaped in the air and screeched like wild Indians, as one might perhaps expect in so barbarian a convention hall as the Wigwam. They had (it was said), as was typical of so uncouth a convention performance, succeeded in nominating "the Baboon." Eastern cartoonists were quick to sketch Lincoln in this role, their pens dipped in acid and prejudice. And the radical antislavery men shook their heads too. Lincoln wasn't the man to be stern enough with the "wicked" slaveholders, who were sure to outwit him.

At the same time, all through the South, men prepared to follow their firebrand leaders. It was now almost a foregone conclusion that Lincoln would be elected, due to the split in the Democratic Party, and they would have none of him. They had been told that he was a "Nigger lover"—forgetting the calm, fair phrases of his speech at Cooper Institute.

Strong winds were blowing every which way. Would nobody listen to the calm voice of reason? Anna Ella Carroll and many others were raising their voices now, voices that were lost in the din. Anne wondered why these hotheads could not see that Lincoln alone among the candidates stood neither for the North nor for the South, but for a whole and united nation that belonged to all of them.

Hers was a reasonable mind. She felt that this was a nation built out of revolution against the tyranny of a British king, built by Washington, Adams, Jefferson, Franklin, and Anne's own kinsman, Charles Carroll, Carroll of Carrollton. These men had risked their necks and often lost their fortunes to give their descendants a common heritage, the United States of America. And now extremists were seemingly about to bring it to destruction.

Divided, the States would become again the prey of Europe and the old regimes. England, defeated eighty-some years ago by the valor of our ancestors, held to a stalemate in the War of 1812, could now easily rejoice that this mad experiment in democracy without the rule of kings and potentates could so easily fall back into ermined laps and servitude.

While the "Wide-Awakes," knowing little but shouting much, marched through the streets of Northern cities in torchlight processions glorifying "Old Abe, our next President"—(and not many of them having the slightest idea of what he was or what he stood for)—others less naive were busily removing much of the nation's supply of small arms to Southern arsenals. Anne was hearing about it all from one Lemuel Evans, who was working in a semisecret capacity for Winfield Scott.

Evans was emphatic about what he knew, even to his reasons why the lovely Anne should marry him right now, before the War. It was, he felt, coming. There was now no escaping it. It was as inevitable as their love for each other. He was a Western intellectual gone from Tennessee to Texas; she was a Southern aristocrat and many other things besides. Caught in all this turmoil, they had found an extraordinary response in each other. . . .

Yet now what time had they, or anyone, for private lives? The long-impending storm was breaking upon the head of the newly elected President, the man who had tried hardest to avoid internecine war, the rail splitter, Abraham Lincoln.

14

"It Gives Me Deep Pain"

The years of foreboding, of the shadowy dread that lurked about the hearths, the doorsteps, and the meetinghouses like a palpable presence, were moving into harsh reality under the ghastly light of November and December days of that year of 1860.

The Republican Party was not committed to abolition, nor was the South, prior to Lincoln's election to the Presidency, committed to secession. But the seeds of dissension, planted through the years by fanatics on both sides, were now about to bear their deadly harvest.

As in all great conflicts, the surface issues that rose to the top of the seething cauldron were given as excuses. They were clearly visible and could be translated into slogans. The South was for Slavery; the North was for Freedom. The South stood for States' rights above the welfare of the nation. It was a vast simplification, or oversimplification, of the facts—the working of economic forces that, like the slow process of erosion through the action of rivers, winds, and rain, finally were splitting the United States.

And now Jefferson Davis was having the effrontery to suggest that Anne and her august father might join the Confederacy! Thomas King Carroll could still exert great influence; he could have a position that accorded with his name. "Not if you gave him the whole South!" Anne made the decision and flung the words into Davis' face.

The atmosphere of Washington was poisonous with the breath of secession and impending civil war. By December, South Carolina was out of the Union and beckoning to her sister states. Before Lincoln had as much as set foot in the White House, Davis was President of the rival Confederate States of America! That included South Carolina, Mississippi, Florida, Alabama, Georgia, Louisiana, and Texas, with more soon to join them.

As March 4 and the inaugural approached, plots were being laid to prevent Abe Lincoln's ever living to take the oath of his office. Working closely with fine old Winfield Scott to protect the President-elect, Lemuel Evans told Anne that they expected attempts at assassination either at Springfield or somewhere along Lincoln's route to Washington. Lincoln was characteristically refusing to take the slightest of precautions, and his guardians were frantic.

Thomas Scott, no relative of Winfield's but a business associate of Anne's as vice-president of the Pennsylvania Railroad, was sharply alert to certain conspiracies fomenting in Baltimore, in "Mob-town." Should the Presidential Special arrive there with Lincoln aboard, wild men with knives were waiting to take his life. He must consent to being spirited through the city in a quite ordinary railroad car in the early hours of the dawn. He finally saw that there was no help for it.

From the very beginning, Abraham Lincoln avoided as much as possible all attempts to give him proper protection, however well meant. He was, perhaps, a fatalist. But, while triumphal arches and enthusiastic crowds had marked Lincoln's progress through the rest of the trip, Maryland's greeting was planned assassination! To Anne's mind, her home state was behaving as disgracefully as South Carolina!

Thank goodness, Lincoln had reached Washington safely and before any guns were fired. If now he could only make the South understand that he was a reasonable man, perhaps war could still be averted. Multitudes were listening as he gave his inaugural address, and multitudes, North and South, were praying.

A month later, Lincoln got his cold answer. With the bombardment of Fort Sumter, all hope of peace vanished. Virginia, North Carolina, Tennessee, and Arkansas left to join the Confederacy and swore to make all-out war.

The heartstrings of the nation were breaking as families were torn apart by their allegiances. Brother prepared to fight against brother, cousin against cousin, friend against friend, in what was to be, proportionate to the numbers involved, the bloodiest war in history.

Since Mr. Lincoln's election to the highest office in the land, Anne had been engaged in a fury of letter writing to her far-flung connections: "Support Lincoln whether you like him or not, he's our only hope!" Now she had, close at hand, the immediate problem of Maryland. Her own family was as divided in its loyalties as the rest of the state. Maryland inclosed, as a nugget to be prized, the District of Columbia. Located on land that originally had been part of the State, the site of the Federal government would fall to the Confederacy should Maryland secede. The Confederate States of America could call itself the official government and be recognized as such abroad.

By the powers, this should not take place! Anne was determined that this could not and *should not* take place. As a mere woman, she could not bear arms to serve the Union's cause. Yet she could call upon weapons far more powerful than rifles and bayonets and howitzers. She had

106

the ardor of her spirit, the acuteness of her mind, her skills as a publicist. And she had the weight of the Carroll name, that—wooed by Jefferson Davis as a symbol of the old aristocracy—could be used with equal force against him and what he stood for.

Groundwork laid earlier by Anne and her father had led to the election of Thomas Hicks as Maryland's governor. Now she would do her utmost to reinforce his precarious stand as a Unionist. Planting loaded articles in the nation's press, Anne sought valiantly to encourage Hicks, warned him to stall for time. "Postpone another meeting of the legislature as long as you can," she advised him. "Give events a chance to work on our side. Let people calm down a bit. If the legislature assembles again, it will almost certainly vote for secession. I have asked around, and I am sure of this. . . ."

And then came one James Randall, to write, to an old German tune, the stirring words of "Maryland, My Maryland!" which said in one version what Anne was saying every day.

Writing Governor Hicks almost daily, Anne remained at her post in Washington. Should she leave the District of Columbia and perhaps join her friend Hicks in Annapolis, other women might panic. Knowing how very close her association with present Southern leaders had been, they would be sure that she was evacuating, that she had had some advance notice of assault upon the capital city. Everyone there was jittery, and even senators were known to be keeping sawed-off shotguns in their offices, ready close to hand.

The whole North was watching Governor Hicks, she wrote him. He must try to stand firm, despite the fearful pressures being brought to bear, while she worked upon public opinion in the state to bring it around to his [or her]

107

side. Time was of the essence, she realized all too well. Troublemakers were inciting Marylanders to open riot, and Massachusetts troops en route to Washington had been attacked by Baltimore mobs.

Could it be possible that John C. Breckinridge, too, was trying to hold his own border state to the Union? Despite her deep misgivings about this Kentuckian, she was forced to admire the courage with which, almost singlehanded, he was battling the rest of the Senate. He had not left his seat, as had others of Southern sympathy; shunned on every side, he might yet be the spokesman for the moderates and the channel through which their voices could be heard.

One could hope against hope that this were so, and that John was not playing a role that, in these halls, was traitorous. Earlier, Anne had asked him point-blank if he were for the Union, and he had calmly said he was. For the sake of his uncle, her dear friend, Anne would in her own mind grant John Breckinridge every benefit of the doubt.

Yet now she heard that Breckinridge was coming to Maryland to try to sway her state toward the South. Right upon the heels of his speech in the Senate which had proclaimed, "A terrible accounting will be rendered by those who are plunging their country into the vortex of ruin under the pretense of maintaining the Constitution!"

John had come out into the open at last. Anne finally knew just where he stood. He was threatening Maryland, her adored Maryland, and she was ready for the fight. Through the suffocatingly humid days of that mid-July and early August, Anne ransacked her files and records and poured words upon paper in what, first intended only as another article for the press, was expanding far beyond such limits. She was determined to write it all down, everything she had discovered through the years, all she had studied and believed.

She was making her astounding *Reply to the Speech of the Honorable J. C. Breckinridge*—now one of our great historical documents. His speech, full of sound and fury, had been delivered before the Senate, July 16, 1861. His premise was tenuous, his lies were dangerous—because many people were apt to believe them and him. He had denounced Abe Lincoln as a despot. He had said on the floor of the Senate that Lincoln had destroyed personal liberties, was taking money from the national treasury unlawfully for the support of an army, and was in fact exceeding all his powers as President. He was, in short, a tyrant who had provoked the war. So said Breckinridge.

So Anna Ella Carroll, a force to be reckoned with, opened up all her guns. She began her *Reply* with what for her was the utmost of restraint. She had read the speech of Breckinridge, she wrote, with deep pain, and with still deeper pain was observing his appearance in Maryland to use "the fallacies of that speech" to stimulate and strengthen the Confederate rebellion. "Evidently his purpose is to incite the military uprising of the people in this State against the Government, in aid of Southern Treason, and to prepare them for action whenever the leaders shall give the signal."

Anne apologized for not acting sooner. "I have in the spirit of friendship, repeatedly repelled by my pen, the charge of disunion heretofore made against him. I could not bring myself to believe that one belonging to a family so illustrious in our annals as his own . . . should at last prove himself recreant to the Union's cause."

Now it was all too clear that Breckinridge, in his very own words, was charging that the "President, in violation of the Constitution, has made war on the Southern States for subjugation and conquest, has increased the army and navy, called forth the militia, suspended the writ of *habeas corpus,* and, without warrant, arrested private persons, searched private houses, seized private papers and effects. . . ."

Harsh words to be used against a small-time lawyer from Springfield! John C. Breckinridge was asserting that the State of Maryland was abolished and that her people were "under the shadow of a broad-spreading military despotism."

Anne, in her historic *Reply,* agreed that these were grave charges. "If true, the President should be made to suffer the extreme penalty of the law." She was, indeed, leading Mr. Breckinridge on, as though in a courtroom argument. Meanwhile dear Leah bathed her throbbing temples and wrists with the fragrant coolness of cologne; Anne was too deep in what was going on in Washington even to think of the soft temptations of the Chesapeake, of the Tidewater. This was no time for vacations.

"The argument turns wholly on the question of *fact,* whether the overt act of treason which the Constitution defines to be levying war against the United States, has been committed? Whether the Confederate States of the South commenced the war?" Anne was now drawing her keen sword from its scabbard. "There can," she wrote with a boiling pen, "be no equivocal position in this crisis; and he who is not with the Government is against it, and an enemy to his country."

She went on. "The major premise of the Senator [Breckinridge], namely, that the President made war upon the South is *untrue,* and I proceed to show that no one in America knows this better than that gentleman. . . ."

It was the time, Anne thought, to reveal to the nation the full extent of the Southern conspiracy made ten years before and clearly revealed in the secret correspondence she had intercepted and shown only to Henry Clay. The multiple letters between the various governors, with places and dates, she quoted, full out. Her *Reply to Breckinridge* was growing into a sizeable pamphlet. Anne would publish it at her own expense, as she did, and in the immediate emergency rush copies the length and breadth of Maryland and even beyond! She would not stop until she had told the whole story. Leah, dear Leah, brushed her fire-red hair, brushed the moist tendrils from the cheek of her adored mistress, or went out to try to find another chunk of ice over which the fans could bring refreshment. With a lump of ice, Anne could cool herself momentarily, even if she could not cool her suite.

"Here," she wrote, "we have every idea on which the conspirators are now acting." The ink on the letters had perhaps faded in the interim, but not the ideas, the rancid, angry ideas, of the men who had written them. And Anne was, and had been for years, on the inside of it all. While some of the writers of the letters to which she referred might be in their graves, their ghosts began to walk with the firing on Fort Sumter. That overt act had drawn the blood that, according to the calculation of certain people, would cement the Southern states into a Union of their own.

"The Southern people back in 1851 would not sustain the leaders in sufficient strength to enable them to carry out their treasonable designs at that period," she went on. Would it were so in these days! "The chiefs of the conspirators went to Washington after the election [of Lincoln] and assumed the direction of the entire treason movement, and proceeded to organize a military force for the purpose of seizing the government, expelling Lincoln, and inaugurating their man Breckinridge."

Anne paused only slightly for breath and a refilling of her inkwell. "In the sight of these astounding facts, the President issues his Proclamation, appealing to the patriotism of the nation for the salvation of the Union, and Mr. Breckinridge grossly insults the intelligence of the coun-

111

try by charging that the President made war against the South!" Anne's legal mind was at work; facts were facts and evidence was evidence. The man Lincoln was all they had to hold things together, and they must work with him. A fragile, human raft in stormy seas!

"The facts adduced establish beyond controversy that the President *did not* make the war as charged, but that the traitors made the war, which now threatens the subversion of the Government, and endangers our national existence. Under this fearful exigency, I proceed to inquire what are the duties imposed upon the President by the Constitution?" Anne proceeded from wide knowledge and deep study to describe them. Since they had been attacked by Breckinridge, and since the present situation was quite without precedent, she felt entitled to interpret the broad terms of the Constitution into particulars, simplified for the average reader.

"The executive power is vested in the President . . . in the event of rebellion or insurrection assuming such proportions as to overthrow the *'republican form of government guaranteed to every State in the Union'* . . . the President is required by his oath of office 'to preserve, protect, and defend' this supreme law. For this purpose the sword, by the Constitution, is placed in his hands. . . .

"The express grant of the *war-conducting* power conferred upon the President carries with it the implied power to use every belligerent right, every instrument known to the law of war. . . . By virtue of the express and implied powers of the Constitution just indicated, it is impossible to question the duty of the President . . . to annoy, to weaken, to destroy the enemy until its armies are overthrown and civil authority is re-established. . . ."

Martial law had prevailed all through the Revolutionary War. Breckinridge was in ignorance to have proclaimed it otherwise. As an earnest student of American history, Anne proceeded to show proof of her points through several pages of this amazing and powerful document. She was leveling her guns, and her fire was accurate and devastating. Her final volley was an explosion of rhetoric:

"Better that Washington had perished like Hampden! That Jefferson had never drafted the Declaration of Independence . . . than that this Union, created to be the *daylight* to break the night of the ages, should finally collapse, and *traitors* be permitted to write the epitaph, 'It lived and died!' "

The words scorched the paper as Anne at last threw down her pen. She had, in the three weeks it had taken her to document and write and revise this epic work, succumbed to the Chesapeake breezes. She was signing it with the proud name of Carroll, in her beloved state of Maryland, August 8, 1861.

15

Advisor to Lincoln

Desperate times called for desperate measures, and lies must somehow be combated with the truth, as Anne saw the truth. She desperately wanted the people of Maryland, her people, to listen—and they did! Hovering at the very brink of secession, they did not, as a state at least, plunge over it. While hundreds of individual Marylanders might join the Confederate armies, the state remained in the Union and was to contribute its fair share to national defense.

Earlier Anne had flooded the state legislators with letters, and she took pains to supply General Winfield Scott with lists of troublemakers to be watched, and if necessary arrested. The cost of printing and circulating her pamphlet, *The Reply to Breckinridge,* was already running into hundreds of dollars more than she had expected to pay.

And now, in this crucial time, Anne's mind was running faster than her own finances could support. With sudden inspiration, she outlined further strategy to her friend Thomas Scott, now Assistant Secretary of War, and her message sent him rushing to the President. The order called for 50,000 copies, and Lincoln agreed that the Government must foot this bill.

The Hon. Mr. Breckinridge had found her "net for traitors" drawing closer and closer, and her reply really unanswerable. Early in September he resigned from the United States Senate and announced that he was joining the Confederate Army. Anne was ready for him; here, she figured, was the time to clinch her argument throughout the border states and farther North. Here was excellent use for the 50,000 copies, and more! Speeding all this literature through the manifold channels she had learned about as a top publicist, now thousands of newspaper editors, governors, congressmen, or others with public or private influence could read it for themselves, could attempt to judge which side indeed was really trying to plunge the nation "into the vortex of ruin."

Anne was, without realizing it, turning out to be a latter-day Thomas Paine, a spokesman for liberty and democracy. To Anne the Union came first, as it had to Clay and Webster. She was out to defend the position of the Chief Executive and his war powers, very remarkably stated in her pamphlet, but at the time it had not really been for Lincoln himself. He was still to her just a figurehead, a symbol, still just an Illinois lawyer who had accidentally been elected to the highest office in the land. He had as yet done little to win her confidence and that of many other thoughtful people.

He was fumbling; the whole North was fumbling. And the first clash of arms between the North and South, between brother and brother, between the Union armies and the Confederate armies in that brutal July of 1861, had been an embarrassment, to tell the truth. Anne, preoccupied with the work on her *Reply to Breckinridge,* had not accompanied the gay folks from Washington who had ridden out to Bull Run, as though it were to a picnic. The battle, presumably won by Union forces at 3:00 P.M. of that broiling afternoon, had turned and had become a horrible rout by four in the afternoon. The senators and their ladies, complete with picnic baskets, were thoroughly upset.

But the South meant business, and no quoting of facts or figures strongly in favor of the North (on paper) could give real reassurance. The population of the Northern, of the loyal states was about twenty-two million; that of the Rebels less than ten million, of whom more than a third were Negro slaves. In fighting men, the North outnumbered the South three to one, in wealth at least two to one.

With such preponderance of power, it seemed to Northern leaders that it should be a simple matter to crush the Rebellion in the space of months or weeks. But Bull Run was shattering to such placid overconfidence; suddenly certain thoughtful people began to grasp the fact that this war might last a long, long time.

Confronted with a thousand confusions, faced with a thousand decisions, Lincoln had read in Anna Ella Carroll's pamphlet an extraordinary clarity of thought and force of logic. She had somehow struck through murk and fuzziness and controversy to come to her essential points, and she had made them stunningly.

While Lincoln and Anne had met socially several times since he had taken office, the President now wished an intensive interview. She was not to wait, his secretary said; Mr. Lincoln was expecting her. Secretary John Nicolay, a rather young and impressionable man, eyed this fashionably dressed, attractive woman curiously—so this was the Miss Carroll everybody was talking about!

Anne herself hesitated on the threshold of Mr. Lincoln's sanctum, not wishing to interrupt an intimate family scene. Little Tad Lincoln was sitting on his father's lap, begging tearfully for a pony. Anne's first impression was—what gentleness this man had! He was cradling the little boy as a mother might. Then she went on into the sanctum sanctorum.

116

"You get younger and better looking every week, Miss Carroll," the President said with his mid-Western twang, as he swept Tad off his knees and rose to greet her. "I can't say the same for this old battered phiz of mine." The deep-set eyes glinted briefly with an innate humor that lightened the essential rugged sadness of his face. "I need your help, and that's the truth of it!"

This man, Anne realized, had no side, no pretense. It was impossible for her not to warm to the simple directness and honesty of his appeal.

"You have already assisted me, perhaps more than you may be aware of!" Lincoln sat back in his armchair, lacing long, bony fingers across his knees. He was dressed in a loose suit of excellent material that looked as if it had never been pressed. "Your *Reply to Breckinridge* is only the beginning of your work for this administration—at least I hope, I most sincerely hope it is!"

Thus Anne was slipped into a role, unprecedented for a woman, as advisor to the President. By Lincoln's express order, she was to have access to the White House at any time, day or night! In an unofficial capacity, she was to serve through the War as practically a member of his Cabinet, moving behind the scenes in wartime, confused Washington, in a position of absolute trust which Lincoln afforded to few of those around him. His actual Cabinet was a spotty one, composed of some dedicated and able men such as Seward, Secretary of State, and others who were questionable and appointed for purely political reasons, such as Simon Cameron, Secretary of War.

While neither side was prepared for an all-out war, the South had the driving force of decision, the gallant devotion to a cause, which was not true of the pedestrian North. All over Dixie the women were sending their men off to war as though to knightly combat in a tournament. How well Anne understood their spirit!

The preparations of the ladies of the South had about them the aura of romance, as they packed hampers with jellies, wines, and confections. They saw to it that their sons, brothers, and sweethearts had inlaid dressing cases, majolica shaving cups, and sentimental little books that quoted from the poets, often with the most tender passages underlined and marked with a cluster of pressed violets. Recalling earlier, happier days, and imbued with the false glory of war, they floated around in their prettiest dresses, daintily marking the boxes "Captain," "Lieutenant," even "Major." They had high hopes.

The women of the North were not similarly ardent. Perhaps they were more realistic. Nor could much be said for the self-seeking gentlemen who descended upon the capital city and upon Mr. Lincoln, to demand officers' commissions or fat government contracts. The city of Washington was overrun, too, with Confederate spies and Southern sympathizers, which was only natural since it was a Southern city to all intents and purposes.

Without her own forthright writings to prove her basic loyalty, Anna Ella Carroll would have been a leading suspect. But Lincoln was a shrewd judge of human nature and of character. He was quick to perceive her immense value, her great potential. Despite the surface graces of her aristocratic background, she was, as he said, "Sassy as a jay bird," a quality he admired. Her general idea was "Let's stop the nonsense, let's name names, and let the chips fall where they may!"

She, too, had a double view of the scene, which, like the stereopticon slides so much in vogue at the time, gave her depth and dimension and perspective.

Part of her Tidewater birthright was an insight into the

Southern mind, and her career had given her a working knowledge of the North and its thinking.

Developing rapidly as a chief executive, Lincoln was welcoming excellent minds and spirits wherever he could find them. Continued stupidity was leading now to heavy losses of time, of money, and of what was far more important to him—human lives. When it actually came to fighting an all-out, great war they were all amateurs, Lincoln no less than his Cabinet, his generals, and army. In what was to be the first of modern, total wars, they had no precedents to guide them.

In the struggle to create colossal military machines almost overnight, the North had the advantage of numbers and materials, the South that of *élan* and the skill of its officers, whose superiority was immediately apparent. Neither side had accurate military maps, and both were dangerously ignorant of where they were going or how to get there. The Government had no topographical information, except for parts of the West, and generals on both sides were planning campaigns from geography tomes they picked up in bookstores!

The Secret Service, a rather formless security organization, was singularly inept; spies were slipping back and forth across the lines, into and out of Washington, with little or no let or hindrance. Talk was loose. Southern agents and sharp-eyed newspaper correspondents, with no particular loyalties except to their papers or themselves, were having a field day. Shockingly uncensored in both North and South, the press was quick to report, without conscience, both the rumor of the day and the actual facts of military movements and preparations.

Starting out with almost no army at all, only 16,000 men in uniform, the North also had few good weapons, no officers well trained in the higher arts of warfare except old Winfield Scott, and an entire order of command as unwieldy as it was out of date. Save for Scott and a few others of his generation, not an officer had ever handled a unit as large as a brigade! A handful of men had fought in the Mexican war, but most had spent their Army careers building frontier forts, "fighting" Indians, or in paper work. As for the rank and file of Northern soldiers, they were farmers, factory workers, city-bred clerks, now suddenly opposed to rampageous Southerners who had lived in the saddle and who were fast men with rifle or sword. Abraham Lincoln himself was a civilian who had served only briefly as a militiaman in a minor Indian war; Jeff Davis was a graduate of West Point.

The military mind, as it showed itself in the Northern forces, was giving Lincoln not much reason to respect it. Informed that a brigadier general had gotten himself captured by the Confederates, along with some horses and mules, the President had said with quiet sarcasm: "I don't care so much for brigadiers; I can make 'em! But horses and mules cost *money!*"

While generals squabbled over seniority and almost everything else, jealousies were also rampant in all branches of the Federal government; and the press was almost universally "ragging" Lincoln and holding him personally responsible for every mistake. Now he came to consult with Anne on many topics and problems presumably beyond the ken of a mere woman.

Her brilliant Breckinridge pamphlet had demonstrated to Lincoln, in a most dramatic way, the value of more information about the war for the general public, something that, at least in modern times, would require a huge staff and a whole floor of the Pentagon in Washington, or Rockefeller Center in New York City. Anne was the staff. This woman could write dynamically, and she knew where and how to influence public opinion, people's thinking. She was well versed in Constitutional law and, like the President himself, was deeply concerned with a quick end to this useless bloodshed. For Anne, the war was a highly personal matter; it was her kith and kin who had already fallen or were about to be sacrificed, on one side or the other.

Exploring many angles of the conflict, Anne spent many hours with her old friend Winfield Scott, Chief of the Army, and still the finest soldier in America. She went over ordnance maps with him, studying his proposed line of attack. Dropsy confined him to his armchair these days, but he was ever the master strategist, pointing out that, as in the little war with Mexico, the place to strike was not around the fringes but at the heart of the enemy itself. "We must divide the South!" he cried, beating the floor with his cane. "And the way to do it is via the Mississippi!"

His was the Anaconda Plan, named after the python. Scott planned to squeeze the South to death. Troops would move down the river and hold it, from Cairo to the Gulf of Mexico. The South would then be cut off from Western beef and grain. Slowly starving, it would be forced to sue for peace. The North would win, without intensive land invasion or attack. Also, this could take years!

No, said Lincoln. Anne agreed. They needed quicker results; the North was growing restive. Yet indeed the muddy Mississippi could hold the key to this vast and spreading theater of war. His attention directed to it by General Scott, Lincoln ordered the shipyards of St. Louis to start building gunboats. The people of the city could no longer snarl that only the East was really profiting by the war and that New England firms were being awarded all of the lush contracts.

All of Missouri was by no means loyal to the Union, as Anne was hearing, with certain vehemence, from her uncle,

Cecil Carroll. For many years he had been a prominent St. Louis lawyer; he was also a deep-dyed Southern sympathizer, and he was sure she had taken leave of her senses in using her talents on the side of the Union. The North had nothing but "a peacock" in command here, he wrote. General John C. Fremont was putting on airs as the former hero of California conquest and making himself and his cause ridiculous.

Lincoln would never find a general to compare with Robert E. Lee. Who did he really have in the field but that pompous ass, George B. McClellan? Anne could almost hear her uncle snorting as she put down his impassioned letters; like all the Carrolls, he had a fiery temper. Anne found herself sighing deeply, because she was in at least partial agreement. George B. McClellan—handsome, impressive, and an excellent trainer of men—was a general who was afraid to fight. The Confederates outnumbered him, he said, again and again parading the splendor of his troops through the city of Washington. He was always complaining to Lincoln that he needed more men with whom to attack, more supplies, more time, more of everything except decisive action on his part. He was still resting on laurels won in the spring, when he had helped the loyalists of West Virginia in their secession from the mother state. A relatively small thing, but he made much of it.

Anne knew as well as her uncle Cecil did that the Government was shaky. Undermined with doubt and the great debts left over from the bungling Buchanan administration, the U.S.A. was considered a very poor risk by the financiers of Wall Street and Boston. France had seized the opportunity, taken advantage of the situation to move into Mexico with an eye toward American conquest. And England, whose mills depended desperately on Southern cotton, was all too eager to aid the Confederacy.

What Lincoln needed was a major victory that would

show the world, and the South, that the Union was still a power to be reckoned with. The North could not only spend thousands of dollars in preparations for war, but it could also fight one. A major campaign along the Mississippi could not afford to fail.

Time was running out—time and also credit. It would not take a good deal more fumbling and lost motion to lose forever the hope of Union that had once been so proudly held. Going its separate way, the South could be followed by the West. Once the pattern of dissolution was set, there could be no end to it, not until the former United States of America lay in fragments, weak, quarrelsome, and an easy prey for the schemes of European imperialism. As Anne herself wrote earlier, its sad epitaph would be carved as on a tombstone: "It lived and died."

She fidgeted in Washington, anxious now to go to St. Louis and see for herself. As for the gunboats, she was a woman raised beside the rivers and hard to fool. The boats, she thought, would take up the least of her time. What she wanted most to do was to talk to people, to get their reaction, to test the sentiment of Missouri, which, from this distance, seemed perhaps to be somewhat similar to that of her own Maryland.

Lincoln could expect scant reassurance from the report of Simon Cameron, Secretary of War. That pompous official had already left for St. Louis, ostensibly to inspect the gunboats but, so his reputation shows, probably just to arrange for a personal cut of the building profits. Pockets were being generously lined by the sale to the Government of out-of-date rifles, shoddy blankets and materials for uniforms which melted in the first rain, of all types of substandard goods— and fingers were pointing to Cameron. He was a man to steal "practically anything except maybe a red-hot stove," acidulous old Thaddeus Stevens had said, and his comment was being repeated the length and breadth of Washington.

Anne was now working on another pamphlet at Lincoln's direct order: *War Powers of the General Government,* actually an amplification of that which she had already touched upon in the Breckinridge reply. She needed time for research—and what was to prevent her from taking it in St. Louis, which had an excellent library? She could use its rare historic documents as an excuse for her exploratory trip. Along the way she could stop at various Army camps, and she would come back loaded with a mine of firsthand information.

A woman could delve without attracting the attention that a man would. No one would suspect that her questions were loaded. She could, if she were sufficiently clever, play the whole journey as a pretty caprice! And she still had the figure, the looks for it.

Weighted down with worry, Lincoln managed a faint smile when she told him her plan. He was eating little and sleeping less, sleeping hardly at all, and the energies and ingenuity of this woman continued to astound him. Anna Ella Carroll could get anything she wanted out of any man, he was quite convinced.

16

Secret Mission

As she planned for her momentous journey to St. Louis, Anne included a riding habit and boots against the eternal mud. She intended to go everywhere in every kind of weather, and refused to be always encumbered by her crinolines. These would not easily pack—all the hoops and silks and petticoats that proclaimed essential femininity but which still left scarcely room for a seatmate beside her in the crowded train cars of wartime. She dreaded the inevitable dust and the cinders and the interminable miles. Most of her excursions, most of her work, had been along the Eastern seaboard, and the West was a fresh adventure.

As a woman traveling alone, she had thought she would perhaps be conspicuous, but now she found with some relief that she was lost in a churning throng. Other girls and women, ladies, were traveling without escort, the wives, the daughters, the sweethearts en route to Army camps and posts and hospitals to join their men.

Most of the ladies were dressed in black. For some these were already widow's weeds, but for most they were merely the practical shade for travel "on the cars." The grimy air and the scene were but little enlivened by the hard-backed seats of green and crimson plush, nor by the audacious cries of train boys starting their worldly careers by selling stale sandwiches and stale newspaper headlines. None of these would go as far as Thomas A. Edison who, at the ripe age of fourteen, was pursuing a simultaneous career on the Detroit-Port Huron run back up north in Michigan.

As the passenger cars were shunted back and forth into side spurs to make way for the crowded troop trains, Anne was crying over the hideous waste and cruelty of war, the loss of hope and dreams, the end of the finest young men. She was seeing the last farewells, the tears of the women, the lads, fresh-cheeked and beardless, leaving home probably forever, with baskets full of fried chicken and coconut cake in their hands.

All that Anne could do now was to reassure her fellow passengers, many of whom had never before been on a train, who clung to their belongings fearing that nameless strangers might snatch everything away somehow in this strange clickety-clack of wheels on track, and of moaning, meaningless whistles. Dressed in their best, the women found their starch wilting. Babies were bawling their little hearts out. Each mother, each of the women, had her personal misery—and her suspicion. Yet they were traveling together, into the night. . . .

It was a feminine world now, peopled only very sparsely by men who asserted their masculinity by excessive chewing and spitting on the floor, a fault noted earlier by European visitors such as Charles Dickens and Mrs. Frances Trollope as evidence of American bad manners. American men chewed tobacco and they spat—as somehow a point of pride.

Anne welcomed the frequent stops and change-overs that allowed her briefly to escape. She could stroll along the platforms during the change of engines or stops for fuel or water or the complete change of trains, hoping against hope that her baggage hadn't been lost. Meanwhile she could sense the glories of October; the land was ablaze with the gold and scarlet of the maples, the abundance of the harvest. They called it Indian summer out here, and said that the purple haze was rising from the campfires of lost tribes, that the corn shocks were the ghosts of Indian wigwams.

Anne was far from the huggermugger of Washington, especially in spirit. Traveling the railroads, she was experiencing anew the sinews of their strength and seeing with new eyes their vital importance. She had often written glibly about them, but now she was seeing how they actually linked the towns of the nation together, how they connected the lamps of lonely cottages and the lights in lonely small-town depots as well as the gaslighted cities. It was really one land, she thought. It *must* be one land, held together by a common devotion.

Stopping off at the various Army camps, Anne found some of her dreamy reveries harshly dispelled. The farther west she went, the more disturbing her discovery that people considered the Union cause all but hopeless. Even its strongest adherents were beginning to despair; the Southern doctrine of States' rights must triumph. Army officers at the military posts were cordial to Anne, but frank. It was a lost cause.

Lemuel Evans, for all his experience in the Secret Service, had not quite prepared Anne for this shock to her dearly held illusions. Perhaps, as her devoted suitor, he had been trying to shield her from these realities. When next they met, she would be furious with him!

Descending from the puffing train into the arms of her uncle, finally actually in St. Louis, she was suddenly back in the bosom of Family. An errant member, perhaps, from some points of view, but still a Carroll. Given a little time, her uncle was convinced that he could make her see the light. She was wined and dined in eminent St. Louis circles;

the people who mattered were as gay, it seemed, as though the fact of war did not even exist!

The ties of blood were strong in the Carrolls, and presumably would convert Anne to the Southern way, the way of gallantry and defiance. Like the powerful, muddy Mississippi on whose banks she stood, St. Louis was deceptive. Sun-dappled and lazy on the surface, it had deep-flowing undercurrents and dangerous snags and shoals.

So it was that fast tongues, unbridled by the wine of social life, were talking freely in Anne's presence—and, being Anne, her ears were always wagging. Albert Sidney Johnston, Confederate Commander in the West, was moving into action so rapidly and forcefully that none of Lincoln's inept generals could possibly stop him—so they said. What matter if Lincoln were building all those ridiculous gunboats?

The important people of St. Louis scoffed at any notion of secrecy or security. Everyone in the city knew about the gunboats. And again and again they assured Anne: "The Confederate batteries will cut them into bits. Send 'em down the Mississip', and that will be the end of 'em!" And there was more to this, Anne sensed, than mere braggadacio.

She determined to cultivate the powerful Mr. Johnston's brother, librarian of the Mercantile Library. Working meanwhile on her new paper for Mr. Lincoln, she had an excellent excuse to go to the library for at least a part of every day. She had met this Johnston socially, and now it seemed that, like her Uncle Cecil, he was concerned with her reform. He could not really believe that a Southern gentlewoman could be so depraved as to support "the Black Republican, Abraham Lincoln."

In the course of heated debates, the librarian revealed more than he knew, or intended to. His brother's forces could not possibly be as strong as he pretended, Anne sensed. He was exaggerating and putting on a good face. As other St. Louisians gathered around and claimed that Missouri would be redeemed and Kentucky overrun by spring, she quietly questioned their protestations.

Yet she listened, too. "The party of peace will be foremost and will demand concessions from your government! These sections will strike for state independence!" they insisted, almost in unison.

"Independence, indeed!" Anne's temper was rising. "Before next spring, the boasted independence of your whole Confederacy will be at an end!"

"And just how," they demanded, "will you reduce the Mississippi?"

Surrounded, Anne fought staunchly back. "Yes, sirs, I predict that before spring, all the strongholds on your Mississippi will have been reduced to rubble, will have vanished into thin air!"

But Anne was assuming a confidence that, in this hostile atmosphere, she did not really feel. Her apprehension of climactic danger was increasing with every day that passed. Lincoln was relying upon the Mississippi strategy to defeat the gallant, well-armed power of the South; and everyone in the know was saying that the river could never be opened, that it was so strongly fortified that it was impregnable!

The flicker of an inspiration came to her. Wasn't there some other way?

She must study the problem, must concentrate, must close her door against interruptions. Lavishly entertained up to now in Uncle Cecil Carroll's house, she must remove to a small hotel to have the needed privacy.

The ornate Planter's House was clearly out of the question. While the most noted, most famous hotel in this part of the West, it had also become a rendezvous for the flashy, for the river-boat captains in town for a brief alcoholic fling, for the gamblers with their cards (and sometimes

their derringers) up their sleeves, and always the specula-
tors, as checkered as their vests. It was hardly a place for
a respectable woman alone. It was not for Anne.

She settled for the modest Everett House and sighed for
dear Leah—Leah to plump the hard pillows and to comfort.
Her only luxury here was a door that she could lock!

Anne was quite alone, except for the impetus afforded
her earlier by Lincoln and Scott, her drive to search through
the maps that she had brought with her from the effete East
and to relate them to present strategy. Unrolling them, she
thought a great deal about Winfield Scott. Many of the
charts and maps she had put together from bits and pieces
were actually more accurate than those the Chief of Staff
had to work with, but they were also so sketchy and dis-
ordered that she would never have thought of letting him
see them.

Any proper Army officer would have scoffed at some of
these hand-drawn projections. Anne had put them together,
acquired them sort of piecemeal, in the course of her work
with R. J. Walker and other railway magnates. The rail-
ways had to have accurate maps. Competent engineers had
charted them in an effort to use the valleys, skirt the mountains, find a level way for railroads through the seemingly
impossible, up-and-down terrain. Many of those projected
railroads had never actually been built, but still the maps
and plans remained on the papers before her, and they
could, Anne realized, mark the route for whole armies!

She was on the ground here in St. Louis, with the Mississippi riddle to decipher. Why she was suddenly focusing
her whole attention upon it, perhaps she could not have
said. She was driven by what, in woman, is called intuition,
and in a man intelligence.

Now, as she spread out these maps and charts, she found
herself recalling other days and other times. She had worked
over all this with Jefferson Davis, and with Stephen A.

Douglas, and there had been a time when it had all focused on Mobile. It had seemed then most important to persuade the extension of a railroad from Illinois to link up with the Southern network. Mobile had always been the spider at the center of that web. Commercial minds had fixed on it, as a sort of North-South control, with easy entrance to the Gulf of Mexico.

Mobile was not on the Mississippi! Here Anne had made an intellectual and tactical break-through, but she was too tired now to go further into the problem. Not today, not tonight!

If only Lemuel Evans were here! She longed for his presence, his advice. He always had a way of calming her, made her feel that being a woman was just as important as trying (usually in vain) to solve the problems of the nation.

But Evans had gone off to Texas on a special mission and, at best, would never find her here. Even if their roads accidentally crossed, he would never contact the Carrolls. Lemuel had his dignity: he knew where he, as an upstart Unionist, would stand with Uncle Cecil.

Suddenly Anne heard a tapping at her hotel door. "Come in!" she said, expecting it was the maid to turn off her light for the night or turn down her bed and expect the inevitable coin. They were always hovering around Anne—the maids and the waiters.

"Lemuel!" she cried joyously, unbelieving! He was veritably an apparition in her doorway. He couldn't be real—but he was.

"Just got back from the Rio Grande. Glad to see me?"

Anna Ella Carroll forgot how much she had wanted to be completely alone; she forgot that at times she had been furious with this man. They were in each other's arms and for that wonderful moment everything, even the war, was forgotten.

17

There Must Be Another Way

How odd it was, Anne thought, that this man with his rough and easy courtesy, his Western forthrightness and directness, could appeal to her heart and spirit more than any of the polished gentlemen she'd known. She was deeply in love with Lemuel Evans. And furthermore, it would be good to have a stalwart man around in this confused and lurid city. Anne was perhaps not quite so brave as she had been trying to make herself believe she was. She was now, out here in the hinterlands, seeing a sordidness, a reality, that had been concealed from her when she was just the protected and cosseted guest of the Carrolls. The streets of St. Louis teemed with soldiers, brawling, drunk; bodies marked with stab wounds were found floating in the river. . . .

And a lone woman, with no obvious business to occupy her or justify her presence in this hot spot, was laying herself wide open to suspicion of being a spy. Impassioned, sectional feelings, inflamed by the red liquor that somehow was always available when food and clothing and blankets and guns were not, could possibly make her the victim of the ruthlessness of the code of the frontier. Tempers were

132

high everywhere. And she wondered whether perhaps dear old Winfield Scott, always protective and kind, hadn't actually arranged for this meeting with Lemuel Evans. Figuratively, she blew General Winfield Scott a long-distance kiss.

Evans had his work to do in St. Louis, and Anne had hers. While they could spend only brief hours together, it was always a comfort for Anne to be able to turn to him, especially on one memorable day. Anne had been horribly unnerved by her sight of the battle-torn Union regiment returning broken, after the battle of Belmont. She had watched the wounded being borne up from the river boats—the boy soldiers so tragically young and twisted with pain, the gray faces of the men who were dying, the bloody bandages, the riddled blue uniforms, and the empty sleeves. Her heart was sick.

"There *must* be a way of escape, a way to end this miserable thing quick and fast!" she told her dear Lemuel Evans. "There just has to be one, Mr. Evans!"

His face was grim. "Might as well give up if we don't find it soon, Miss Carroll. Won't take much more fiddling around for Napoleon and his French to grab Texas."

Forms of address, even between sweethearts and husbands and wives, back in the 1860's, were formal and stiff. It was always "Miss Carroll" and "Mr. Evans," in spite of their close relationship.

Yet now Anne was somewhat in despair. What could she go back and tell Mr. Lincoln about his cherished Mississippi River plan, except that it could not possibly work? Lemuel Evans, with his insight, was confirming everything that her Southern friends and contacts had told her, and adding details out of his own firsthand knowledge. The Confederate forts along the big river were well-nigh impregnable and could rake the new gunboats with their batteries. Anne had

133

also discovered that the speed of these expensive new craft would be only five miles an hour, under full draft. Even if they could take advantage of the current, they would be sitting targets. Once crippled, how would they have the power to make their way back upstream?

Anne had increasing doubts about it all, but, being Anne, she checked first with the river pilots. Because it seemed to her that the gunboats, and the brave young men aboard them, would fall into the Confederate's bag like mallards at a gun shoot. It just didn't make sense.

The chill of early November was penetrating everywhere, and especially along the great river, as Anne, dressed in the riding habit and boots she wore for these muddy waterfront excursions, trudged wearily along the streets that led to her small hotel. She had shed the airs of a society belle along with her crinolines, and somehow it was a relief not to have to pose as the important Miss Carroll now—with her heart heavy as lead.

Her talk with the river pilots, the horny-handed men with the know-how, had been informative—and shocking. Almost to a man they had said that they would rather be shot at sunrise than take the helm of one of those fancy gunboats. "If we want to die we can handle it better some other way, better than taking fool orders from some fool of a general who don't know nothing about the old Mississippi, and that's a fact, lady!" In other words, they took a dim view.

Politicking with her father since her earliest girlhood, Anne had learned that the best way to get information was "straight from the horse's mouth." Men who made their living by running the river were not apt to be far off the beam on anything concerning the Big Water. They had no foolish theories in their heads.

Still, Anne told herself sagely, there was a bare possibility

134

that the men she had interviewed had all been Southern sympathizers. It had been beyond her to check or sense their actual affiliations.

Returning from her trip to the wharves, Anne became suddenly aware of approaching footsteps behind her in the gathering dusk. She quickly turned and was relieved to see that it was a woman, and not entirely a stranger. Anne, in her busy career, had met many people—this little fuss-budget of a woman was somehow familiar to her—had it been in Washington or Baltimore?

The pursuer stopped short. "You have a man who's still out with General Grant?"

Anne held, and the woman came closer and introduced herself breathlessly as Mrs. Charles Scott, another occasional guest at the Everett House. Her husband was a river pilot, and she was desperately worried about him.

"Is he loyal to the Union, then?" demanded Anne, getting down to cases and realities.

Mrs. Scott was vehement. Her man had had a whole boatload of precious cotton ruthlessly confiscated by the Confederates, and he hated them with his whole heart, and so did she.

What a stroke of good fortune! Anne wondered—could she actually talk to this man, on his next return home? She had ideas. She suddenly wanted to know the depth and width of *all* the Western rivers. "For certain!" Mrs. Scott nodded. She went on to say that her husband was a good man to ask if anybody wanted to find out about rivers; he knew more about all of them, large and small, than a catfish!

Again that night Anne pored over her maps, as if perhaps a fresh idea might arise from them. She was used to seeing reality from symbols such as these, used to seeing hills and rivers and valleys exemplified on a chart. And it

135

made her angry and humiliated to realize that crafty Jeff Davis was now using these lines, these railroads, that she herself had helped to promote. For the first time in history, railroads both of the North and South, transporting troops and supplies, were the actual arteries of war!

"But the Mississippi *can't* be the only possible way." The thought kept dinning in her fertile mind. "There has to be something else!" But where to find it? What other course could really divide the South, sever the railroad life line of food and other supplies that were flowing across from Texas? There must be a way to strangle the great General Lee and his gray armies. As Anne, bent over her hotel table under a feeble gaslight, let her glance run over the map, it happened to fall upon the Tennessee.

She gasped with inspiration. Could this be the answer, or perhaps, as an alternative, the Cumberland? No, the Tennessee! According to the map before her, the conquest of the Tennessee River could, if properly planned, do everything that was being expected of the Mississippi Plan—and could do it even better and with far less loss of lives. The Tennessee was not strongly fortified and it flowed to the north! No wounded gunboat need fall into Confederate arms during an engagement, it could drift back with the current to safety.

The Tennessee, Anne felt, was almost too good to be true! From it, an army could readily cross overland to the Tombigbee and then, descending it, capture the major Southern port of Mobile itself! The Tennessee opened a route all the way from Illinois to the Gulf of Mexico; it could command the whole valley of the Mississippi. With this area under Union control, the war that Anne so abhorred could speedily be brought to an end.

Daylight had long since faded, and the gas jet was beginning to sputter petulantly overhead as Anne started scribbling maps of her own. She had always enjoyed drawing maps; as a child it had been one of her dearest sports to figure out on paper, mapwise, the best route to get from where she was to elsewhere, from this plantation to another plantation, or the crossroads, or anywhere. Now those early, childish flings came home, in a sense, to roost. The times were moot. And Anne realized that nobody else had even thought of hinging a whole plan of strategy around the Tennessee! There was a war on, a terrible, destructive war that must be speedily concluded, and could it be possible that nobody else, none of the military geniuses, had even touched on that possibility?

In her excitement, Anne had still to fight off doubts which—like mosquitoes—kept singing about her auburn head. The Plan, the Great Plan, was becoming so clear and obvious to her that indeed there must be *something* wrong with it!

How could a mere woman see what experienced military men had not? Who was she, Anna Ella Carroll, to pit her mind against the dignified deliberations of a dozen generals? But, she reminded herself, "Old Marse," General Robert E. Lee, was running circles around the Union leaders. Yet were the "Rebs" really so much smarter than the "Federals"—the "Yankees"? The honest answer, at least so far in the conflict, had been "Yes"!

Anne had no pretensions as a military strategist, but she had learned much from Winfield Scott. She had long emerged from the silly conventions that restricted all, or almost all, of the women of her era. Circumstances had forced her to fight her way into making a living in a man's world, had forced her to think about new problems in a masculine way. She was also a stubborn, embattled patriot.

137

When the actual existence of the nation was at stake, it was the solution that was important, not the means. Whether a man or a woman had found it—no matter!

Her concept was unconventional and extraordinary, just as Anne herself was. Working far into the night, she was step by step unraveling the knots that existed or might exist, smoothing out the whole piece of strategy. She was convinced that this attack, this plunge, would be successful, and that the river Tennessee could be the road to victory and peace.

Up to now the devoted, inspired Southerners had taken and kept the initiative. The Union armies had been largely on the defensive, getting there latest with the leastest. But a real surprise attack . . . ?

Was the Tennessee deep enough to take the gunboats? How far up was it really navigable? Was it equally navigable in every season of the year or only during spring and summer freshets? These were deep and vital questions which only an experienced river pilot could answer. She would not even ask Lemuel Evans; she dared not even raise his hopes until she was sure.

And her busy mind hit upon Pilot Scott. She had met his wife. The good woman had said that her husband knew all the "Western" rivers, but that could have been an exaggeration. What about the actual Tennessee, the neglected river that flowed the wrong way? Anne rushed out of her room and down the corridor to check. In her eagerness, she had forgotten how early in the day it was; and she hastily apologized for her intrusion when she was met at the Scott's door by a flustered lady still in her curlpapers and wrapper. But no real matter—Mrs. Scott looked happy at the call, and, as one woman to another, asked her in—and changed the subject to ask Anne's advice about a new coiffure! Curls, maybe, or bangs here? She finally settled down enough to say that her husband, the pilot, was presumably safe and would be back tomorrow. Of course he had worked the waters of the Tennessee! He knew it like he knew his own pants' pocket!

So Anne must cool her heels and wait. She waited with considerable impatience for this all-essential conference with Scott, but meanwhile she sat down and worked out further ramifications of The Plan. Politically, she saw, it could have an immediate effect. She was of course well aware that the farming interests in the eastern part of Kentucky and Tennessee were loyal to the Union and opposed to the upsurging planters farther west. Action in this sector would perhaps encourage an uprising. Farmers are notoriously slow to heat—and slow to cool!

When the summons to meet Charles Scott—veteran river-boat pilot— finally came, Anne was trembling. What would he say? What this experienced man might tell her could dash her ingenious expectations to pieces. It was a strange but important interview. Like most of the river-boat pilots with whom she had talked, Scott had only scorn for the Mississippi project. He was, she was quick to see, a rough and crusty individual who obviously knew his business, who was irritated at having it interrupted by a war, and who deeply resented generals so full of their own brass and spit and polish and stars that they never asked the advice of common folk—the folk who knew whereof they spoke.

"The Tennessee, ma'am? Now you're talking sense!" Scott hit the table with a heavy fist. "It's deep enough; boats can run clear up the stream to Muscle Shoals in Alabama." It was deep enough for gunboats in any season of the year, he told her solemnly. One could, however, count on the Cumberland for only part of it. All rivers differed.

Excusing herself hastily, Anne ran to fetch Lemuel Evans from his hotel room down on the next floor from hers. Suddenly she felt the need of masculine support. She was but a woman, after all! And Evans could think of many vital questions to ask the very responsive Charles Scott that she herself could obviously not. Tugging at his elbow to make him hurry, like a little girl on the way to the candy store, Anne managed to disclose breathlessly to him the whole story of The Plan—she had hit upon the Other Way!

Many years later, Lemuel Evans, who had become Chief Justice of the Supreme Court of Texas, was to tell the whole story in an official statement to the United States Senate:

When he [Scott] stated to her that in his opinion, and in that of pilots generally who were familiar with the western waters, that the naval expedition could not open the Mississippi; that the gunboats were not fitted to fight down the river, and that it was practicable for them to go up the Tennessee [it confirmed her idea], that the Government should direct the Mississippi expedition up the Tennessee River to some point in Northern Mississippi or Alabama so as to command the Memphis and Charleston railroad.

In a very earnest and animated manner she [Anne] communicated this thought to me. Being a native of that section, and intimately acquainted with its geography, and particularly with the Tennessee River, I was at once impressed with the tremendous value of her suggestions. She immediately introduced Captain Scott to me, with a request that I would interrogate him on all his special facts. He stated the number and strength of the [Confederate] fortifications on the Mississippi and the impossibility of gunboats to reduce them, the width and depth of the Tennessee River, and the practicability of ascending with the gunboats to the foot of Muscle Shoals, but did not think they could pass above.

With the view of ascertaining the practicability of a naval expedition to reach Mobile and ascend the Alabama and Tombigbee rivers, I questioned him [Scott] as to the depth of these waters also. We were so impressed with the fullness and accuracy of his information, that Miss Carroll asked him to write it down for her, to do which he declined from want of education, but finally consented. . . .

In conclusion, I will state that having critically examined all the plans of our generals and everything official which has been published by the War Department on this point and every history which has been written upon the war, it is evident that up to the time Miss Carroll submitted her plan to the Government it had not occurred to any military mind that the true line of invasion was not down the Mississippi, nor yet up the Cumberland to Nashville and then overland, but that it was the Tennessee River, and on that line alone, that the Mississippi could be opened and the power of the rebellion destroyed.

What a woman this was! Lemuel Evans looked down at her tenderly, back in that little hotel room in St. Louis. They had finished their momentous, their history-making, interview with Pilot Scott. And there was Anne, Anna Ella Carroll, a lovely woman standing amid strewn maps and charts, a little white and strained, perhaps, with all this thinking and planning of a way to end a war she never wanted. But the eyes that sparkled into Lemuel's were as radiant as the springtime bluebonnets of his own Texas.

"THEATER" OF THE TENNESSEE PLAN

Note how simple and logical it all was after Anna Ella Carroll
had the genius to figure it out and supply the plan of strategy
that won the Civil War.

18

The Great Tennessee
Plan

Anne lost no time in sending off a letter to
Thomas A. Scott in Washington, the only man
in the War Department that anyone could really
trust. Lincoln had just sent old General Winfield Scott into honorable retirement and had
replaced him with George B. McClellan, a feeble reed to
lean upon if Anne had ever heard of one! Affairs in Washington must be frantic, she thought. And the quicker she
got back there, the better.

Her letter, however, gave Scott only a slight inkling of
her scheme; she dared not entrust more than a hint to the
mails. It seemed inadvisable to write her complete report
while in St. Louis; she would keep the gist of it safe in her
head, where there was no chance of rifling or intercepting.
Spies were literally everywhere. Letters, even official letters,
were opened. Anne had good reason to suspect that someone with access to her rooms at the Everett House was
methodically going through her desk drawers and her
wastebasket.

She had written to Thomas Scott largely to pique his
curiosity, and also to reassure him that she was going
through official channels and not straight over his head to

the President, as she could easily have done. Scott had an acute brain; he was actually running the War Department, and his co-operation and enthusiasm could carry a good deal of weight. Anne knew, from bitter experience, how edgy men of authority could be, how jealous of their hard-won positions.

She stopped off briefly in Ohio to discuss some of her general ideas with old Whig friends and associates—men who were leaders still, and loyal—but extremely dissatisfied with the Administration's ineptness. They would support her plan if need be, and so would Millard Fillmore, still a power to be reckoned with.

But now to set her plan down on paper. She would draw up her full account back in the calm of Tidewater, she decided. There she could go into semiseclusion. No one need know officially of her return, and there at home she would have none of the interruptions that she would have to face in Washington.

Back to Baltimore she came. But to her dismay, Anne discovered that gloom and despondency had settled down like a heavy fog all over the East. Thanksgiving this year was a travesty, and the gathering at the Carroll family board was small. With her brother's medical practice suffering severely because he was a Unionist, and several of her sisters so strongly "secesh" that they scorned any pretense of family reunion, the Carrolls who remained offered the traditional prayers with a lump in their throats.

The document upon which Anne was engaged might well change all of this. That was her avowed and devoted purpose; to end this inter-family war! She did not dream that with it she was to place herself among the great heroines of history!

She had decided that she must present her proposition from two angles. Mr. Scott, as Assistant Secretary of War,

144

a former business executive and transportation authority, must be won by incisive statements backed by facts and figures, while Lincoln himself would be quick to grasp the political and military significance of what she was so earnestly recommending. Above all, she must be brief. She had long ago learned, as a public relations woman, to study her clients and to anticipate their reactions. And now, as she reviewed her journey to the West, "with a view of making my own observations," she was drawing upon hard-earned experience and waging her own special form of psychological warfare.

Here in her own words: *

In the first place, the Civil and Military authorities are both laboring under a grand mistake in regard to the true key [to attack]. It is *not* the Mississippi, but the Tennessee River.

It is well known that the eastern part, or the *farming* interests, of Kentucky and Tennessee are generally loyal; while the middle and western parts, or what is called the planting districts, are in sympathy with the traitors.

Traitors, such as John C. Breckinridge, she thought but did not add. Her blood boiled at the very thought of his still being a power in old Kentucky, in the State of Henry Clay!

But except in the extreme western parts, the Union sentiment still lives. Now all the preparations made by the military in the West indicate that the Mississippi River is the point to which they direct attention. On that river heavy risks must be incurred, and many battles must be fought, before any impression can be made on the enemy.

As Anne wrote this, the faces of the mortally wounded men and boys she had seen in the St. Louis military hos-

* From *The Tennessee Plan*, by Anna Ella Carroll, courtesy The Maryland Historical Society.

pitals rose to haunt her . . . the sobs of the women, the smell of death everywhere. . . .

All of this could be avoided by using the Tennessee River [as an avenue of attack] which is navigable for medium-class boats to the Mississippi line, and is open to navigation all the year, and the distance is but 250 miles by river from Paducah [Ky.] on the Ohio.

The Tennessee River offers many advantages over the Mississippi; we should avoid the almost impregnable batteries of the enemy, which cannot be taken without great danger and loss of life to the assailants, from the fact that our boats, if crippled, would fall a prey to the enemy by being swept by the current to him, and away from the relief of their friends.

But even should we succeed, still we will only have begun the war, for then we shall have to fight to the country from which the enemy derives his supplies. [Anne had explored the situation from every conceivable angle.] Now an advance up the Tennessee River would avoid all this danger; for if our boats became crippled, they would drop back with the current to their friends, and escape all danger.

But a greater advantage still is that its tendency would be to *cut the enemy's lines in two* by reaching the Memphis and Charleston Railroad, threatening Memphis, which lies 150 miles due west, and no *defensible* point between; also Nashville, only 90 miles northeast, and Florence and Tuscumbia in north Alabama, 40 miles east. A movement in this direction would do more to relieve our friends in Kentucky, and inspire the loyal hearts in east Tennessee than the possession of the *whole* of the Mississippi River, and if well-executed would cause the evacuation of all those formidable fortifications on which the rebels have grounded their hopes of success.

Here Anne was coming to the very heart of the matter. Attack by way of the Mississippi would amount to banging their heads against a stone wall. The alternative that she was proposing would lead to reducing the enemy forts *from*

146

the rear! A fig for all the fancy phrases of military parlance. And a pox on one-way, obtuse thinking. A civilian mind like Mr. Scott's might have the imagination to see the whole scope of her plan, and so, she hoped, would Lincoln's.

And in the event of our fleet attacking Mobile, their presence [loyalists in Kentucky and Tennessee] in the northern part of the state would be material aid to the fleet.

Again, the aid they would receive from the loyal men in Tennessee, would enable them soon to crush the last traitor in that region, and the *separation of the two extremes* would do more than a hundred battles for the Union cause.

Anne's whole analysis must be as graphic as words, charts, maps, and diagrams could make it. As Leah came and went unobtrusively to keep the fire glowing in the grate and a pot of tea at her mistress' elbow, Anne measured distances on the maps with a pair of calipers until her lovely head began to ache. It was Leah who scolded Anne into eating, and it was Leah, finally, who turned off the gas jet night after night and ordered her mistress to sleep. "No use to make you'self sick, Miss Anne."

But Anne wrote:

The Tennessee River is crossed by the Memphis and Louisville railroad and the Memphis and Nashville railroad; Hamburg, where the river makes the big bend to the east, touches the northeast corner of Mississippi; entering the northwest corner of Alabama and forming an arc to the south, enters the State of Tennessee at the northeast corner of Alabama and if it does not touch the northwest corner of Georgia, comes very near it.

Anne had double checked with her notes from Pilot Scott and from Lemuel Evans.

It is but eight miles from Hamburg to the Memphis and Charleston railroad, which road goes through Tuscumbia, which is two miles from the river, and crosses it at Decatur, 30 miles above, by the road intersecting with the Nashville and Chattanooga Road at Stephenson.

She was trying to give Scott, and Lincoln, the whole picture of the transportation network; her calculations were concise and intensive.

The Tennessee river has never less than three feet to Hamburg, on the shoalest bar, and during the fall, winter, and spring months, there is always water for the largest boats that are used on the Mississippi river. Hence it follows, from the above, that in making the Mississippi, or rather overlooking the Tennessee river, the subject is not at all understood by the superiors in command.

There! Her Tennessee Plan was all down on paper, under the date of November 30, 1861. If they did not understand its implications now, heaven help the nation! Drained by her concentration, Anne was exhausted when she finished setting this down on paper. The journey from the West had been arduous, and she had rested scarcely a moment since her return home. While dear Leah soothingly brushed the tangles from her auburn hair, disarrayed as always when she worked, Anne wished with all her heart that it could be equally simple to unsnarl the affairs of state!

Without some slight breathing spell, she could not hope to regain her presence, her usual buoyancy, nor to be in shape to cope with Washington and its convolutions. She must not, she would not, let herself succumb to the general mood of discouragement! True, the government was near bankruptcy, spending nearly two million dollars a day, and had an army and navy that seemed inclined either to loaf or to lose.

So it was not until a few days later that Anna Ella Carroll was ready to gird herself for battle and breeze into the sacrosanct War Department. Travel-weary, as she had been a few weeks ago, she could not have faced Scott or anybody; now she was ready to face a hundred lions in any arena! Bigger and better lions, indeed, than this man who sat across the desk from her! He had so changed in her absence that she was shocked. Naturally aggressive and full of force, Scott had shrunk into himself with an air of hopeless listlessness that covered the room like dust. He seemingly could not believe that there was hope anywhere, and he told her so.

"But I insist that you listen to me!" Anne stamped her pretty, gaitered foot. She was a woman, playing a man's game. But she drew all her maps and papers from her muff, with the inference that if Mr. Scott did not care to look at them, she would take the whole packet straight to the White House. She hadn't really been on vacation. Hadn't Mr. Scott read her note from St. Louis?

"Well then," he smiled faintly at the recollection of earlier encounters with this ball of fire, this Anna Ella Carroll, who was indeed something to be reckoned with when her cheeks were flushed.

As Anne began to read from her report, she could see a quickening of his interest. Bombarding him with facts, figures, logistics—and the force of her own personality—she quite destroyed his apathy. He was now asking pertinent questions; his facile mind was getting at least into second gear.

"Miss Carroll, I believe you have come up with a solution to the entire problem!" He whipped the papers from her grasp and studied them with heightening excitement. "I can't see a flaw!"

With scarcely a by-your-leave, he flung a coat about his shoulders and sped away to the White House. Anne crossed her fingers.

19

Name the Master-Mind!

Years later, Scott was to describe the impact
of Anne's Tennessee Plan upon a sorely pressed
Lincoln, a President trying to carry a super-
human load compounded of anxiety, vicious at-
tacks from the newspapers, and the delays and
demands of his fumbling generals. It was this man who
had said humbly only a few weeks before, after being
snubbed by General McClellan who had gone coolly up to
bed while Lincoln waited in an anteroom to see him, "I
will hold McClellan's horse, if he can only bring us some
successes!"

Which McClellan hadn't and didn't and never would.

But as Abraham Lincoln reviewed Anne's brilliant plan
of strategy, an expression lighted his face that Scott was
never to forget; he had never before seen Lincoln show
such pleasure as he did at her deft and ingenious solution
to the great problem of ending the war. Hope, joy, and
relief flooded the deeply etched lines of his roughhewn
countenance; and from this hour, Scott told Anne, Lincoln
could "think of nothing else."

The miasma of despair that had settled over the capital
city was like the evil breath of a sodden swamp, or worse.

150

With the turn of the year, Senator Wilson of Massachusetts expressed the general attitude when he said before the assembled Congress: "Why, sirs, you can be borne all over this country upon the wave of popular murmur against the Government . . . it springs from the deep disappointment of the people of the country who have poured out 500,000 men and hundreds of millions of dollars and see no results! They see no policy in the administration of the country; they see no plans; they read of no victories."

As supreme commander of the army and navy, Lincoln had reserved for himself the control of the Mississippi expedition and had been waiting only for the building of the necessary gunboats to embark upon the operation. Now Anne was turning his mind, for the first time, into another direction. The information with which she had supplied him was so complete and clear and her arguments so logical, that they knocked the props out from under the earlier scheme. Yes, she was only a woman. Women did not plan military strategy. Yet she was a woman in a million, and Mr. Lincoln was wise enough to sense it. She was right. It was the Tennessee that could well lead to the victory that would revitalize the sagging North.

Scott confirmed this; it was the only way. Lincoln had unbounded faith in this man's knowledge of the railroad system and its potential use in the pursuit of the war. Anne had given him grounds for equal confidence. Making the crucial shift of operational planning from the Mississippi to the Tennessee took courage, but Lincoln made his decision and took immediate steps.

First of all, it was imperative that the notoriously inefficient Simon Cameron be ousted from the War Department and be replaced, as Secretary of War, by Edwin M. Stanton. Stanton had political backing, and he had ability and drive. Whatever Lincoln's personal feelings about Stanton might

151

be, they must yield to the good of the nation. Lincoln had ample reason for his dislike and distrust; it was Stanton who had, not many months ago, remarked publicly upon the "painful imbecility of Lincoln," and had frequently referred to him as "the original gorilla"!

Nervous, tempestuous, contradictory, domineering—Stanton was all of these, and yet he was a whirlwind of energy. The War Department could use him, and Lincoln pressed for his appointment. Thomas Scott must be left to move about more freely, with the idea that he would go to the West and increase the effectiveness of the army there against the coming thrust.

Beyond Stanton, Scott, and tough, dynamic Ben Wade of Ohio, chairman of the newly created Congressional Committee on the Conduct of the War, few other officials were to know that the whole new concept known as the Tennessee Plan was the work of a civilian and—what was even more incredible—of a *woman!*

It was at the time all top secret—as secret as the Manhattan Project of a later time. But Lincoln sensed the need for the utmost secrecy and caution, especially about the origin of the plan. The bare truth would demoralize the army and the North; the South would jeer. Imagine a petticoat general!

The wheels had begun to turn, but now Anne—aware of how easily they could stall or reverse their direction—pointed out to Mr. Lincoln that there was no reason whatever to wait until spring. Now or never! She was in close contact with Pilot Scott, whose wife wrote his letters for him since he was illiterate, ignorant in everything but the ways of the waters. Passing further information on to Thomas Scott, she added notes of her own to increase the sense of urgency and to keep her cherished plan in the foreground, as on January 10, 1862:

152

Some weeks ago, on my return from the West, I gave you my views of the *Tennessee river* [assault] as being the true key to overcome the rebels. That river is never obstructed by ice at any period of the coldest winter; while every year the Mississippi and Cumberland rivers are impeded by ice. Besides, the gunboats are not well fitted to retreat against the current of the western rivers, and as their principal guns are placed forward, they are not so efficient against an enemy beneath them. They have either to fight with their stern-guns, which are only two, or else they must anchor by the *stern,* and thus lose all advantage of *motion,* which prevents the enemy from getting their range. Anchored, these boats present a target, and the enemy will not be slow to improve the benefit. . . .

There is no difficulty [in navigating the Tennessee] throughout the year. . . . Whoever will look at a map of the Western states can see in what a position *Buckner* [famous Confederate general] would be placed, if we would make a strong advance up the Tennessee river. He would be compelled to back out of Kentucky, as, if he did not, this force could take Nashville in his rear and oblige him to lay down his arms.

In spite of her optimism about a drastic change in the fortunes of the North, Anne was beginning to take a long look at her own financial situation. She had shelved most of her other projects to work for the Union, but her high status in Administration circles was so unprecedented as to be vague, to say the least, in terms of actual income. Unlike the present day, when the President has a special fund, accountable to nobody, for emergency use, the situation then was that financially Mr. Lincoln's hands were somewhat tied. Anne had received some $1200 for her *Reply to Breckinridge,* which was barely enough to cover the cost of the thousands of copies that had been printed and distributed.

As a businessman, Thomas Scott was troubled about this, but all he could tell her was that: "It was understood that the Government would treat her with sufficient liberality to compensate her for any services she might render."

These were fine words, but they would not pay her bills. All she had seen in actual cold hard cash was $1200. The financial affairs of the government were in chaos, she knew. And she also knew that millions of dollars were going into graft. Manufacturers and go-betweens were making their fortunes. The contrast was a bitter one. Common soldiers in tattered, shoddy blue uniforms were dying in the camps from dysentery and neglect, while new-made millionaires were adorning their ladies with diamonds and egret plumes.

The enlisted men were giving all they had. Could Anna Ella Carroll do less? Should she go on? While her reason advised "No," her whole temperament, her warm and patriotic heart, said "Yes!"

During those difficult days of winter, 1862, she stilled her various doubts and anxieties by completing her work on *The War Powers of the General Government*. Primarily, she was stoutly defending Lincoln against the accusations of "despot," but she was also defining what had never yet been made clear. What actually *were* those powers? The fathers of the American constitution, as on many other vital points, had been vague.

Anne worked too hard and cared too much. Lemuel Evans, stopping off in Washington occasionally from his various missions to the West, tried to soothe her. She found comfort and solace in his arms. With him at her side, she could ignore also the increasing and obvious slights from Mary Todd Lincoln. The President's wife saw in Anne everything that she herself desired to be and was not; she was viciously determined to make Anne pay for her hard-won prominence in government and in Washington society.

Which is probably the real answer to many things. It could not have been just because of "security regulations" that Anna Ella Carroll's real role during this crucial period in the nation's history should have been kept secret for so long. Was it "for military reasons" or because Abraham Lincoln had an insanely jealous wife? An attractive, brilliant, charming woman who could see the President at any hour. . . . Mary Todd Lincoln, insecure, disturbed, would make the most of innuendo.

Coming into her room before one of the White House receptions and pulling on his gloves, Lincoln would ask, with his usual merry twinkle: "Well, Mother, whom shall I talk to tonight? Shall it be Mrs. D——?"

"That deceitful, stuck-up woman? No, you shall not listen to her flattery!" Elizabeth Keckley, the intelligent mulatto modiste who had become Mary Todd Lincoln's confidante and only true friend in the loneliness of the White House, had an attentive ear and recorded what she heard and remembered, for posterity. Scenes like this were an everyday matter in the Lincoln household.

"Well then," said the President, "what do you say to Miss C—— [meaning Anne]? She is too young and handsome to practice deceit."

"Young and handsome you call her!" Mary Todd was in one of her furies. "You should not judge beauty for me. No, she is in league with Mrs. D——, and you shall not talk to her! I do not approve of your flirtations with silly women as though you were a beardless boy fresh out of school!"

She took her husband's arm as they prepared to descend the great staircase and meet the colorful assemblage, while Elizabeth Keckley watched and listened. "There is Mrs. D—— and Miss C—— in particular," continued the shrewish First Lady. "I detest them both. They are the ones I insist that you ignore."

The leaders of Washington society had not included

Mary Todd Lincoln in their invitations when she had been the ambitious, pushing wife of an obscure congressman from Illinois. The wounds rankled, and Mary Todd was determined to make these ladies suffer now, in any way she could.

Had Mary Todd but known, receptions and teas and protocol were the farthest things from Anna Ella Carroll's mind at the moment. They were a hollow mockery in this time of war. What was real and important was that it was February of 1862. Her Tennessee Plan was taking form in terms of an actual military campaign. The gunboats were moving, not down the Mississippi as the Confederates expected, but up the Tennessee! They were escorting shallow-draft steamboats that carried eighteen full Union regiments under the command of Brigadier General (Hiram) Ulysses S. Grant. He was not at the time a very illustrious figure. According to all reports, he had been a failure most of his life. Though a graduate of West Point, Grant was known to the people of St. Louis as an itinerant who had been peddling firewood to them at $10 a cord. He had drifted on to Galena, Illinois, and when the war broke out, had been selling cowhides. His income, at best, had been $800 a year—in a good year. He had been on his uppers.

The South had little to fear from a nonentity such as Grant. How could one compare him in the same breath with "Marse Robert," the great, brilliant, patrician Robert E. Lee?

Grant was an inarticulate man, who could express himself only in action. And in action he did, a great contrast to the vacillating, timid McClellan. His action sounded with a dit-dit-dash upon the telegraph wires leading east. With land and river-borne forces working together, the gunboats shelled Fort Henry. As Anne had shrewdly predicted, the defenses of the Confederates along the Tennessee were weak. Union troops readily marched in and took the flag. Any other Union general of the time would have rested upon this victory, but not U. S. Grant. The main body of the Rebs was fleeing overland twelve miles to Fort Donelson on the Cumberland, and Grant methodically pursued them.

All this proof of her pudding made Anne's heart race, as she heard the reports. The tide was turning!

It was characteristic of Grant that he should count little upon the support of the Upper Mississippi fleet in the attack on Donelson. Even in the assault upon so feeble a fortress as Fort Henry, the gunboats had proved themselves to be unwieldy. Many had been disabled, and only the upflowing current had saved them from capture by the Confederates. They would obviously have been pulverized if the action had taken place on the Mississippi, as originally planned.

Grant was methodically settling in for a serious land siege, with 27,000 men in blue. As balmy weather turned to mid-February blizzard, the men were almost freezing where they stood. Not daring to light fires for warmth for fear of disclosing their positions, soldiers huddled together at night, tried to find shelter behind bushes, and by light of day pulled the triggers of their rifles with fingers that stuck cruelly to the metal. Grant had but one idea: to strike hard and brutally, and this he did.

Anne was with Lincoln and Stanton in the telegraph office of the War Department when the dispatches began to arrive. Thomas Scott had left, a week or so ago, to implement work in the West, with these parting words to Anne: "This is your plan, and if it succeeds, the glory is yours!"

But she was not looking for glory. Anne was tense with apprehension. So much was at stake! So much could go wrong! Stretched out wearily on the couch he so often used when pushed beyond his strength, Mr. Lincoln clearly expected the worst. There had been so many disappointments. It was hard for any one of the three people gathered here to believe that the first telegrams did not hold out false hopes.

The pauses between the messages from Donelson were long. The receiving instrument was silent now, and the operator had even taken off his shoes and gone to sleep. It was high time, Anne thought, that she followed suit. Donelson must have been another defeat chalked up to the Northern cause.

Suddenly the instrument came alive and with it the telegrapher. Translating the Morse code of the wires with a hasty scribble, he came to them with hands that shook. General Simon Bolivar Buckner, the Confederate general in command of the defense of Donelson, was asking Ulysses S. Grant for terms of surrender!

The North had its first real, resounding victory, and it had come so swiftly that the listening three in Washington were all but overwhelmed. And it had come, amazingly, along Anna Ella Carroll's proposed lines of attack. Less than two weeks after the day the troops had embarked upon the campaign, two forts had fallen to the Union forces, with a minimum loss of life and 13,000 prisoners! Sixty-five guns, some of big caliber, had been captured, along with a vast store of sorely needed small arms.

A blast upon the trumpets of Jubilee. . . .

Good news, at long last! Men rushed from stores, from countinghouses, to join the marching bands in Northern cities. Schools recessed. And women knelt in cathedrals and little churches in thanksgiving. Bells rang. Cannon thundered. The spirit of civilians and soldiers alike zoomed like the rockets that burst above the flames of buoyant bonfires. Maybe soon it could be all over!

The Union was now sure of Kentucky and was thrusting

a strong arm into Tennessee; it had advanced 200 miles into the huge domain of the Rebels, and was now beginning to slash at Confederate vitals. And behind it all was an auburn-haired (the gold had tarnished but slightly with the years) woman who had worked it out on paper, who had planned every move of it, because she believed, as had Webster and Clay, in the essential rightness of the Union. A patriot, she.

Few knew how this had actually come about, but the dramatics were there. The North exulted, and the South panicked. What master-mind had detected the weakness of the Confederate flank and, refusing to attack the armored main body, had directed the sword to the point where the South was least protected? Who had perceived that the Tennessee and the Cumberland were as vulnerable as the underside of a terrapin?

Writing to Lee upon the heels of this disaster, the Confederate Secretary of War, Judah Benjamin, cried: "The heavy blow which has been inflicted upon us by the recent change of operations in Kentucky and Tennessee renders necessary a change in our whole plan of operation." Soon Benjamin was to declare that "our entire force must be thrown [away from the seaboard] toward the Mississippi for the defense of that river and the Memphis and Charleston Railroad."

The eminent Confederate historian Pollard was to report later, from the perspective of the years: "The fall of Donelson broke our center in the West."

Whose was the master-mind? In South and North the question was on everyone's lips. Who was to be feared or to be crowned with laurels?

Was it perhaps Henry W. Halleck who, as Commander in the West, had scarcely emerged from his office in St. Louis to take any action at all? Newspaper reporters, flocking to interview him, found him as confused as they were by the sudden turn in events.

Was it Grant? He was still a subordinate, following orders, although he had certainly executed them with surprising precision and force.

Certainly it was not the hesitant George B. McClellan who, with his enormous and inactive Army of the Potomac, was still safe and snug in winter quarters just outside of Washington, talking big, doing nothing.

Everyone was playing a guessing game, and none could come up with an answer that really fitted. Why hide the name of one who was obviously entitled to the highest honor and acclaim? Who had planned the first real Northern victory? Congress would insist that it be revealed.

20 | Silent Woman in the Gallery

For days and even weeks, the halls of Congress had been invigorated by an excitement they had not known since the beginning of the war. Knots of busy people clustered about men who were supposed to have inside information, which usually led nowhere. Rumors fluttered like sea gulls; rumors which mostly had no confirmation. Even through the clouds of cigar smoke, it was clear that some strange new power, some remarkable brain, was at work. The victory had obviously not been pure happenstance. It had been part of an all-over plan that showed the stroke of genius.

Washington was a disturbed anthill. The empty-headed were quick to leap into the vacuum and to try to win favor with their constituents by offering gratitude and formal thanks to names picked almost at random, to various fuddy-duddy generals, to favorite sons, and even, in an excess of overt enthusiasm, to such figures as the fanatical Clement L. Vallandigham, the leader of the traitorous Northern Copperheads. Someone must be named, if only for the record. The *real* someone never was.

The more responsible people in authority visited Mr. Lincoln in the form of a delegation, and they were met with a blank "No." "Public service requires secrecy," was all that the President's spokesmen could or would tell them. Everything was under control, and the facts would come out later.

From time to time, a certain woman rustled into the visitors' gallery of the House, and, perhaps playing a bit nervously with her bracelets, reviewed a scene which had in it some of the elements of farce. Should she step out and reveal herself; should she make a point of taking the lead in what might turn out to be one of the great dramas of the age? What thoughts, what wonders, must have been racing through the mind of Anna Ella Carroll in those days! As the author and creator of The Plan, she was now the newest and most brilliant major general in the army, and an obvious sensation for the sensational press.

Dear Lemuel Evans and dear Thomas Scott were urging Anne to insist upon recognition of her achievements *now*, while the burning light of victory and glory might even erase "the shame of sex." Edwin Stanton himself wanted to speak up for her, in Congress or anywhere, and Ben Wade had agreed so heartily that he wrote her a note, which is part of the record: "Your services were so great that it is hard to make the world believe it! That all this great work should be brought about by a *woman* is inconceivable to vulgar minds. . . ."

Yet even now Mr. Lincoln still refused to give the official permission that would raise the curtain of silence. Just as her inborn code of honor kept Anne from breaking her word to the President, so innate decency and compassion made the whole inner circle, the People Who Knew, withdraw from further pressure upon a suddenly stricken man, pushed beyond his strength.

Twelve-year-old Willie Lincoln was dead.

The bright little boy, most lovable and promising of any of the Lincoln lads, had succumbed to "a series of complications," accompanying what doctors of today would have readily diagnosed as typhoid fever. The medical science of the time was, to say the least, primitive. There was no penicillin; there were no antibiotics. And the anxious care of both parents was not enough.

Abraham Lincoln reeled under this cruelest of blows, and Mary Todd was so unbalanced by her grief that the President had to lead her to a window in the White House and point out to her, a shape gray but still distinct, the outlines of an asylum for the hopelessly insane.

So the flags of triumph, the first real triumph, were whipping in the wind all over the North as the flag over the White House slipped to half-mast.

Abraham Lincoln. Husband and father. President—of what? Lincoln knelt before the casket. The blue-eyed, high-spirited boy was gone forever. And Anna Ella Carroll watched, through her flowing tears. There was a ceremonial funeral, and the circle of foreign ambassadors were politely concerned; the members of the Cabinet were sympathetic—all the great and powerful were making an appearance that could not compare in effect, in real sympathy, with that of Lincoln's neighbors and friends back in Springfield, Illinois. How meaningless all pomp and circumstance! A little boy was dead.

"Might God give this man the strength not to stagger and fall under the burdens that have been placed upon him! God save the nation. . . . God save us all!" Anne prayed.

And she, for one, would not add in the least to the load that the tall, gaunt man was carrying. Not in this precarious time. Her old friend, Roscoe Conkling of New York, was fighting to keep the pages of history open for the insertion of her name. He was now introducing a resolution in the halls of Congress to the effect that his fellows be not too quick to erect lofty statues to gilded gods until the true facts, and the names of the true heroes, of the War were known.

Whatever Lincoln's faults and omissions, he would be honest and just to her in the end. Anne must try her utmost to believe this.

The clouds of glory, however misty and obscure, were beginning to come to rest on Lincoln's head. He had never desired this, but people generally throughout the North, for lack of any other alternative, were already placing laurel wreaths there. The astounding victory, and the plan that lay behind it, *must* have originated in his brain! There were other, shrewder minds who saw that the whole conception of the Tennessee Plan more probably came from someone close to him; Lincoln had given no previous signs of being a military genius.

Despite his stature and his many virtues, Lincoln was also an astute politician and as such quick to seize the advantage. He would not use this psychological moment to exalt a woman, but to demote the popular general who had long been a thorn in his flesh. McClellan must go! He had been entrusted with the fate of all the Northern armies and he had failed in that trust. The soldiers adored "Little Mac"; and housewives had his handsome countenance in colored chromos upon their kitchen walls as a sort of reassurance, a father-image. Yet McClellan was not a panacea, not a remedy for what ailed the nation. He was, to put it bluntly, a general who was too timid to fight.

The main trouble was that George B. McClellan had "the slows," as Mr. Lincoln expressed it. He had given the North excuses instead of victories. Always exaggerating the number of Confederates that faced his troops, he had constantly demanded more—more men, more horses, more guns, more of everything.

Lincoln was almost always disgusted and confused by the military mind; now, for the time being at least, he would dispense with the military geniuses, and he himself would pass upon major military plans and formulate strategy. According to the Constitution, the President is Commander in Chief of the armed forces. And he had at his elbow the woman who had outsmarted all the generals, North and South, an ample reason for his confidence.

The morale of the Northern armies was suddenly at an all-time high. And Mr. Lincoln, rallying from his deep personal sorrow at the loss of his beloved son, was moving into that month of March, 1862, as a leader who would brook no opposition.

Not even from Anne! With the entire Tennessee campaign so clearly outlined in her mind, she had scant concern for the other important theaters of war. Her rooms at home were lined with maps; they fell in skeltering upheaval from behind the gilded mirrors of her private life and for a time thoroughly obscured it.

On to Vicksburg! Its fall, she believed, would mean more than the taking of a hundred Richmonds. With the South unnerved by the first blow to the solar plexus at Donelson, it could be staggered by rear assaults upon its major Mississippi fort. The Union forces must move quickly and take Vicksburg by surprise! Perhaps the war could be over in the early summer! Was war, like the sea, to be made of women's tears? Already the slaughter, the list of dead and wounded, was incredible, fantastic. No other war in recorded history had higher casualties.

In October of that year of 1862, Anna Ella Carroll was still reminding Secretary Stanton of the basic concept inherent in her original plan. She had outlined it and turned

165

it in almost a year before, but the follow-through on it had faltered, following the desperate and bloody battle at Shiloh, in April.

Anne wrote:

As I understand, an expedition is about to go down the river for the purpose of reducing Vicksburgh. I have prepared the enclosed map to show more clearly the obstacles to be encountered in the contemplated assault. It is impossible to take Vicksburgh from the front without too great a loss of life and material, because the river is only about a half mile wide, and our forces will be in point-blank range of their guns, not only from water batteries lining the shore, but from those that crown the hills, while the enemy will be protected by the elevation from the range of our fire.

By examining the map I enclose, you will see why a place of so apparent little strength has been able to resist the combined fleets of the Upper and Lower Mississippi [New Orleans had fallen]. The most economical plan for its reduction now is to push a column from Memphis or Corinth, down the Mississippi Central railroad to Jackson [capital of the State of Mississippi].

The occupation of Jackson and the command of the railroad to New Orleans would compel complete immediate evacuation of Vicksburgh, as well as the retreat of the entire Rebel army east of that line. . . . With regard to the canal, Vicksburgh can be rendered useless to the Confederate army upon the very first rise of the river; but I do not advise this as Vicksburgh belongs to the United States, and we desire to hold and fortify it. The Mississippi River at Vicksburgh and the Vicksburgh-Jackson Railroad will be necessary to us as a base for future operations. Vicksburgh might have been reduced eight months ago, as I then advised, after the fall of Fort Henry, and with much more ease than it can be done today.

The war, to Anne, was a sort of gigantic chessboard, but she had little or no patience with the slow moving of the pawns. It was time to risk the queen and move the chief weight of the Northern army to the west, to achieve the fall of Vicksburg and make directly for the Gulf. It would take years and torrents of spilled blood to prove that, even before the war was eight months old, she had put her dainty, feminine finger on the checkmate move. The North could win only by cutting the South in two, and she—a woman, a socialite, a publicity writer—had clearly pointed out the simplest way to accomplish this.

While Anne's was the master-plan and basic concept that, in all essence, would be followed by the Union generals who finally crushed the gallant South, she, being only a woman, was forced to sit back and watch and listen while others eagerly claimed credit for her work and her plans. Like many another complex problem suddenly dissolved by some ingenious invention, the simpleness and essential value of her Tennessee Plan were so evident (after she had formulated it, and it had begun to work) that military geniuses who had earlier glimpsed only fragments of the concept, limited to driving the Rebels from Kentucky and Tennessee, demanded title to the whole. They contradicted each other to the point of the ridiculous. Everybody had dreamed up Anne's plan except Anne herself!

The generals were flying kites, and Lincoln could at any moment cut their strings. Yet somehow he wanted these military men to feel that they were doing the whole business of saving the nation. Let them squabble; the truth would come out later.

Meanwhile, Anne's continuing work for the President continued to be a well-kept secret. There was only an occasional slip. One evening, when a group of congressmen were conferring with Mr. Lincoln in the White House, they were interrupted by a messenger sent by Anne. Fingering the note the boy had brought, the President turned and looked out of the window. Through the murk and beyond the lanterns in the far distance that marked the tents of the Union forces was the looming shadow of the Confederacy. Speaking almost to himself, Lincoln said: "This Anna Ella Carroll is the top of the Carroll race. When the history of this war is written, she will stand a good bit taller than ever old Charles Carroll did!"

What did he mean? She was just a busybody Washington society woman, wasn't she? Only one of those present was in the know, and he reported the incident to Anne, thinking that it would please her. It certainly did. But she had reason to wish that Mr. Lincoln would also soon see his way clear to flatter her in a financial way!

21 | Tapestry of War

In her mind, Anne could hear always the distant, menacing rumble of cannon. Some day they would be silent, and what would happen then? Was it possible that any ultimate good could have been achieved by this unutterably horrible war that, like an insatiable demon, was devouring the lives of the finest young men on both sides—and the spirits and the hearts of those they had left behind them? Even if the Union could be saved, the peace could still be lost.

As Anne pushed aside the pile of unpaid bills that had been rising steadily upon her desk, the future had become almost as great a concern as the immediate present. Literary endeavors for the government were now pouring steadily from her facile pen; articles of war information for the general public, letters to the newspapers, memoranda to the War Department, and now a pamphlet entitled *The Relations of the National Government to Revolted Citizens,* published late in the spring of '62.

With Mr. Lincoln, she was exploring the problems of reconstruction, already being faced in some of the border states; her pamphlet was a reply to Senator Charles Sumner, who led the antislavery radicals. His was a vindictive group, insistent that the Rebels be made to eat the bitter bread of defeat, that Lee and Davis should be hanged "on a sour-apple tree," that all property of Rebels should be confiscated as punishment for their treason! But this was expressly forbidden by the Constitution, as Anne herself succinctly pointed out, setting forth Lincoln's views as well as her own:

"Peace can only be restored to the country by extending to the people the shield of the Constitution. The Union of these states cannot be restored under a mutilated Constitution, or a different one."

The radicals were also being insistent that Negro slaves throughout the South be freed by immediate proclamation, but Lincoln refused to be pressured. It would be a grand, theatric gesture, but also a hollow one, if the slaves were given nothing save their technical freedom. Few of them had any place to go, any work to do, anything at all but the existing pattern.

Listening to Anne's tales of Patty Cannon and her calculated horrors, and of the desperate plight of human beings freed only to become the prey of the unscrupulous, Lincoln was now working with Anne on a plan for a Negro colony, probably in Central America. Here the Negroes could achieve true independence. Like Liberia in Africa, this was a long-cherished dream of humanitarian Southerners like Anne's father; and now they thought that the day was coming when it might be realized.

It was, as we can see from the perspective of later years, completely unrealistic. The American Negro, by this time many of whom were part white or even mostly white, was not equipped for his ancestral jungles or any other jungles. He was somewhere halfway in between savagery and civilization. He was not ready to go out on his own.

But it seemed on high levels that a proclamation was the first step in the right direction, and that others must follow. Writing and rewriting his Emancipation Proclamation, Lincoln was not ready to deliver it to the nation until January of 1863.

As the nation alternated between hope and despair through the weary years of the internecine war, so Anna Ella Carroll herself flickered. She had been borne into the shining clouds by the Emancipation Proclamation which clearly defined this holocaust as a real war for freedom, but she was also having to face continually the grueling realities of service without pay. Mr. Lincoln had promised that "she will be taken care of," but—preoccupied in many other directions—had as yet done nothing about it.

Her bill had now mounted to $6250, much of it for printing and traveling expenses Anne had paid from her own pocket; but all the War Department felt they could pay her now, without an embarrassing special warrant from Congress, was $750!

It is possible that Lincoln assumed all Carrolls were rich. Often entertained at the Washington mansion of Anne's somewhat remote Carroll relatives, he observed the smoothly oiled machinery of the aristocratic household. He did not pause to consider that there Anne, like himself, was only a guest. To the homespun lawyer from Illinois, Anne was a great lady. Certainly she carried herself like one and dressed to suit the part.

Lincoln's experience of women was limited, to say the least. He had had a very vague and tenuous love affair with Miss Rutledge and had managed to reach her bedside as she was dying. He had married the pushing, ambitious Mary Todd. To judge by his own wife, the only woman he really knew, women were all frivolous and extravagant. They ran up bills behind their husbands' backs. Perhaps because Mary Todd Lincoln spent hundreds of dollars adorning her charms with such gowns as her rose moire antique with pearls at the throat, it is possible that subconsciously he could only put all women, even Anne, into the same category. He could not see, and only another woman and a catty one at that, would note that Anne's ball gowns had been twice remade (by clever Leah) and that she was now replacing her jewels with roses.

Manlike, Lincoln, for all his inner sweetness and understanding, could also be harsh and quick in his judgments. He seemed neither to know nor care that Anne had *never* been an heiress, that the family fortunes had failed, and that she had really been making her way for herself and for her family since she was less than twenty years of age! She had protected her slaves and personally had managed to free twenty of them at staggering expense. She had depleted her resources in trying to hold the family plantation together, and now she had no income.

Lemuel Evans was still urging her to marry him now. After the war, they could go on down into Texas and seek a fresh fortune. Anne loved him, but if she could only make him understand why she must still refuse him! Love of one person for another was one thing, but she was involved with giving the whole measure of her devotion to her country.

Women everywhere had been drawn out of the orbit of their personal lives to meet this terrible emergency. And while some of them might be on the government payroll, as Anne was not, the desire for selfish gain was farthest from their minds. Women, of both the North and South, were giving the last full measure of devotion.

Mary Livermore, bright, sensitive, and—with her husband—editor of a Chicago journal, was tending the wounded and writing of a suffering that found its duplication in almost every battlefield. She wrote:

Hundreds who fell at the beginning [of the attack on Donelson] when the ground was soft and muddy were frozen to the earth and had to be cut out of the ground. Their removal was torture, as few ambulances and wagons had springs, and jolted and pitched them down from the precipitous heights where they had lain two or three days in their bloody and frozen uniforms. Hundreds died miserably before relief came to them. Surgeons . . . . were few in number and medical supplies were utterly inadequate to the occasions.

Gentle Dorothea Dix, famous for the pioneering work she had already done to give the mentally disturbed humane treatment and understanding, to end the "snake-pit" approach, had been called to duty at the age of almost sixty in order to try to bring arrangement into the hit-and-miss corps of hospital nurses. Dauntless Clara Barton was on the battle front, close behind the firing line, doing all that was within her power to pick up the wounded and care for them tenderly, regardless of whether they wore the Union blue or the Confederate gray. And it is part of the record that quaint "Mother" Bickerdyke cruised the battlefields at night, refusing all rest until she had assured herself that no man remained alive and unaided among the fallen.

No, Anna Ella Carroll was not the only woman who stood up to be counted. Along the home front, women were the driving force of the newly formed Sanitary Commission, and in the great cities of the North they were arranging fairs that raised millions of dollars for sorely needed medicines, supplies, and convalescent homes. Also, women were more and more taking the places of the absent men in factories and on farms.

Inspired by two great leaders in the cause of women's equality—Elizabeth Cady Stanton and Susan B. Anthony —women everywhere were undertaking the monumental task of securing hundreds of thousands of signatures to petitions urging that the Emancipation Proclamation be made the law of the land. The Constitution must itself prohibit slavery, now and forever! In the ringing words of these leaders: "When a mother lays her son upon the altar of her country, she asks an object worthy of her sacrifice. In nursing the sick and wounded, knitting socks, scraping lint, and making jellies, the best and bravest may weary if the thoughts mount not in faith beyond and above it all. Work is worship only when a noble purpose fills the soul. . . ."

Anna Ella Carroll was not alone among her sex in devotion to the cause; women, on both sides of Mason and Dixon's line, were giving their all. Slipping back and forth between the lines in various disguises, women were among the cleverest and most daring of the spies, the espionage agents. Even if caught, chivalry would be apt to prevail on either side; a lady was a lady, and thus not likely to be hanged.

Nowhere was courage more heroic and more marked than among the women, the ladies, of the South. With the grimmest determination, they were fighting every inch of the way with their men, their sons and husbands and brothers and cousins. Turning bright faces to loved ones on leave, dancing and flirting in their old party frocks, they still tried to present the outward appearance of the belles men liked to see. Drawing upon their scanty supplies, they were sending the very best that they had to the front—cabbages now, instead of fancy dressing cases, no cakes, but bread baked from grain that someone had walked miles to carry and have ground into flour. The women were making shoes and uniforms, making medicines from herbs, and they were now improvising hospitals in churches and schoolhouses. They were infusing the men they loved with their own indomitable spirit.

It was so both in the South and in the North. In the bloody tapestry of a war riddled with intrigue, corruption, and needless suffering, the names of thousands of women, known and unknown, still stand out like shining threads of gold. Each was in her way trying to stanch the wounds of a land that was bleeding to death. And things would never again be the same.

22

April Can Be Cruelest

As Anne sat night after night in the telegraph office of the War Department, usually with Lincoln and Stanton and Wade, to catch the latest dispatches from the various fronts, she could see the outlines of her original strategy for the Western armies now vivid, now obscured, taking form and fading, all too often thwarted by jealousies among generals vying for place and prominence, by retreats and withdrawals to "previously prepared positions." The fortunes of this terrible, internecine war were parlous and uncertain still.

With maps and charts and logistic plans spread out before her, she was now working most closely with Ulysses S. Grant, the nobody-general who had come up from nowhere to make some sense in the almost senseless situation and who was now undertaking the siege of Vicksburg. And Vicksburg, it was increasingly apparent to Anne, could only be taken from the rear. She had tried to point this out more than a year before, when the North could have taken the fortress with the shock value of surprise.

Anna Ella Carroll was, as history proves, a military strategist of the first rank, even though she was not a graduate of the military academy at West Point. And President Lincoln knew it.

But Anne had to cope with General in Chief Charles Halleck, known as "Old Brains," though he seldom joined her and Lincoln and Stanton in their nightly vigils. A scholarly and self-satisfied man, General Halleck was generally presumed to have great strategic ability; and he took pleasure in basking in the reflected glories of the actual victories of Grant and of the effective Tennessee Plan originating from a noncombatant, a civilian, a woman! Surly and gruff, tactless and overbearing, he had soon become one of the most unpopular and disliked officials in wartime Washington.

Lincoln had been plagued with pompous military men; the South was rich in leaders like Lee and Jackson and dozens of others. But while ineffectual Northern generals peppered headquarters with telegrams, this "brain trust" did not hear from Grant for anxious days. Perhaps, being realistic, he expected his actions to speak louder than his words. But there were gossips and irresponsible newsmen who presumed to say that his silence was due to his intemperance. Mr. Lincoln took a dry view of that; everyone knows his remark: "If I knew what brand of liquor Grant drinks, I would send a barrel of it to every other general in the field!"

As a matter of fact, there is nothing in the records to show that Grant was an alcoholic, or that he drank more than anyone else might have done under the circumstances. That whole story is legendary, and the indications would seem to prove otherwise. Newspapermen of the time were at a loss for personality stories; they made them up with slight regard for ethics.

The ancient horsehair sofa in the telegraph office was perhaps a sort of haven for Abe Lincoln, a man pushed almost beyond his strength but somehow rising to every occasion. There he was away from the cold grandeur of the White House, from his nagging and neurotic, perhaps psychotic, wife and from memories of his son Willie. Stretched out on the sofa, in the cozy warmth of the telegraph room, his roughhewn face would sometimes lose its mask of weariness. Anne, or one of the other devotees, would wake him from his nap to bring the important news. Important news from Grant, if at all. None of the other generals had much of good news to report.

At that time, the War Department was but a short-cut, a block or so away from the White House. Yet the way there was lined with trees and thick shrubbery, a source of concern to the Secret Service, who were charged with the President's safety. Mr. Lincoln's casual habit of walking that way alone, at any hour of the day or night, was well known to the public. An assassin could easily lie in concealment in the bushes. But Lincoln shrugged away all warnings. The Rebels would gain little or nothing by getting him out of the way, he reassured his would-be protectors. And if they were actually determined on killing him, they would manage it anyway.

Anna Ella Carroll and others close to the President did not agree. He should, they insisted, take more reasonable precautions and not continue to tempt fate. He was insisting, too, on taking long, unguarded walks and drives all over the capital city whenever the mood moved him. It was his whim, his preference, in those trying days.

But the tides of war had brought a rabble to the gates; Washington was now overcrowded with all sorts of strangers. Few were as innocent and pathetic as the displaced "freed" Negroes who had come expecting somehow to find Sweet Beulah Land, the wonderful land of promise. In their childish but understandable confusion many of them counted on Mr. and Mrs. Lincoln to be the benevolent

"Massa and Mistuss," heads of the plantation. They were bewildered and lost when it turned out otherwise. One old colored mammy complained that though she had been here in Washington for eight months, "the Mistuss," meaning Mrs. Lincoln, hadn't even given her so much as a shift, or change of underclothing! Yet the basic trust of the majority was touching, and those who had talked with or even glimpsed Lincoln said that "he walk de earth like de Lawd."

Lincoln was deeply concerned by all this. Whatever would become of these poor trusting souls, victims of a "war to make men free"? What of the displaced persons, the ragged deserters, the soldiers hobbling along on stumps for legs? Sometimes Anne hid her eyes as she was driven through the streets.

As that bitter year of 1863 moved into summer, terrific battles were raging in the East as well as the West. And then two victories on one momentous day, the fourth of July. After a six-month siege, Vicksburg had surrendered to Grant, and the great "Marse Robert," General Lee, was finally retreating before the overpowering forces of General George G. Meade at Gettysburg. Should Meade pursue the shattered Confederate forces, the rebellion might soon be ended and the desperately awaited peace be at hand. It was a consummation devoutly to be wished, but it was not to be.

As church bells rang and rockets of victory burst into the Northern air, a jubilant crowd in Washington pressed Lincoln for a speech. He had just been driven in by carriage from his summer retreat in the country; but on this occasion he was, for him, curiously offhand and noncommittal:

"I am not prepared to make a speech worthy of the occasion."

Lincoln went on to praise, in general terms, the men

who had fought so valiantly and who had seemingly turned the tide. He went on to say: "I dislike to mention the name of one single officer, lest I do wrong to those I might forget. Recent events bring up glorious names, and particularly prominent ones, but these I will not mention."

Anne felt the color rising in her cheeks as Mr. Lincoln hesitated in his impromptu speech. Was he at last about to give her publicly the recognition so well earned and so long overdue? But he stumbled on to an ending that puzzled the press and everyone else except Anne and her intimates. "Having said this much—I—I will now take up the music."

The military band, taking this as a cue, struck up with full fanfare; if the President had intended to say more, it was drowned out by the blaring of trumpets.

General Meade did not seize advantage of the opportunity and take off after Lee. Meade, as Lincoln said in disgust, was acting "like a duck hit on the head." Grant, on the other hand, was losing no time in reorganizing his army for the drive on to Mobile, the final point in Anne's far-reaching and farseeing plan of 1861. He was thwarted in this by Halleck, who outranked him, and was forced instead to march his troops off to the relief of Chattanooga. "It would have been an easy thing to capture Mobile at the time I proposed to go there," Grant was to write later in his memoirs. He could then have attacked the enemy from the rear and inflicted, in his own words, "inestimable damage upon the country from which his [Bragg's] army and also Lee's were yet receiving their supplies." The words were almost a paraphrase of what Anna Ella Carroll had said earlier.

"I was so much impressed with this idea [the Tennessee Plan in Anne's presentation] that I made several requests to be allowed to follow through on it." The entire approach had opened his mind to strategy on a grand scale, instead

180

of limiting battles to a confined and limited scale, as heretofore.

Anne watched and waited, during those dark days, as the stars of other Northern generals faded and Grant's steadily rose. Despite malicious comment in the press, despite overt requests for his removal, Lincoln stood firm; he could not spare this man. "He fights!" the President said. Ulysses S. Grant had come to stand for "Unconditional Surrender."

Grant was Anne's idea of a fighting general, as he was Mr. Lincoln's. No matter how he looked, and usually he looked like an unmade bed. Brady's pictures of the time show the general as short and unprepossessing, whiskery, disheveled. He was scarcely the public concept of the spit-and-polish military leader. But he got the job done. It was not until March of 1864 that Lincoln called him to Washington and gave him supreme command of the armies of the North.

Anna Ella Carroll was as usual at the weekly White House reception when a sudden hush fell over the clickety-clack of tongues. At the entrance to the East Room she saw a stubby man in a seedy, unpressed uniform, lacking some of its insignia, who was chewing nervously on an unlighted stogie and obviously very much embarrassed at the attention he was receiving. This was General Grant, who had arrived unannounced and unheralded. He had the look of a man who would rather take Vicksburg again than face the men and women from Washington high-level society and politics who swarmed at him from every side. According to all reports, it was a hullabaloo. Hoopskirts were crushed and feet were trampled and even tables and chairs were overturned. Grant hastily retreated, as he had never retreated before the Confederates. Finally he stood on a sofa, where with his slight stature all could see him even if they could not grasp his hand. He was the "belle of the ball," and hated every minute of it.

Anne was formally introduced later to this upcoming military genius with whom she had communicated so often by telegraph. With her master-minding in Washington, and him in the field, they had between them generated and put into action the electric force field known as The Tennessee Plan. Grant's eyes, like hers, were blue and resolute. It was a time for resolution.

As the war approached its later phases, the slaughter grew ever more tragic and tremendous, wasting the best of the young men on both sides—if not on the battlefield, in the prison camps. The wharves along the Potomac were glowing with the ghastly lights of the hospital ships bringing back the casualties, the broken and maimed bodies left from the battles of the Wilderness. It seemed to Anne that the grim procession of ambulances would never stop, and that peace would never come while an able-bodied young man remained alive in either North or South. And if nerves were now at the breaking point in Washington, what must it have been like in Richmond?

How could the Confederacy hold out so long? What spirit her beloved people had and how sad the consequence! Anne thought much of this, being a Baltimore belle and seeing both sides of the conflict. The forces of the South were dwindling; old men and beardless boys were feeble reinforcements. The railroads of Dixie were so worn that they were all but useless. The supplies of the South were so cut off by blockade of the ports and strangulation from the West that they were close to exhaustion. And yet the gallant South fought on.

Anne could not keep from shuddering as General William T. Sherman marched to the sea all the way from Atlanta, ravaging the heartland of the South, spreading terror and flame. The South might come to concede defeat, but its people would never forgive this shock to the noncombatants, to the women and children, this burning of the ancient homes, this pillage and rape. The North was leaving scars that would never heal. Anne knew her South; she knew the poison of hatred that would seep from generation to generation.

She was continuing her day by day work with the President on the many-headed hydra of reconstruction if and when; it had to be planned on a tremendous scale. She had further explored the unprecedented constitutional and legal angles in her pamphlet, *Rights of the Seceded States;* and, while her earlier contributions of thousands of dollars in time, money, and skill had not been repaid (and never were), at least at long last a way had been found to put her on salary. She had a special niche in the Department of the Interior, albeit three years late.

Somehow, 1865 held hope of a gentler spring. Lincoln had given his second inaugural address, this time with no fumbling. He closed the message with the unforgettable words: "With malice toward none; with charity for all; . . . let us . . . bind up the nation's wounds; . . . care for him who shall have borne the battle, and for his widow, and orphan—to do all which may achieve and cherish a just and lasting peace . . ."

Anne was also deeply disturbed about the growingly ominous threats against Lincoln's life and against those of his inner circle. Anne herself had received numerous anonymous notes warning her that she would pay for her role as "traitor to the South"; since she was a semiofficial member of the Cabinet, she had to share the very real danger. Yet she held to the thoughts Lincoln had expressed in the inaugural speech; it was what she felt in her inmost heart. Anne had with the years come to have a new concept, a new understanding, of this uncouth rail splitter from Illinois. The man had grown right before her eyes, slowly, gradually, naturally.

The redbud and the dogwood were blooming now; the air was soft with April; and gallant General Lee was surrendering his sword to Grant at Appomattox (who handed it back, in tribute to an adversary worthy of that steel). The cruel war was all but over. The terms of surrender, at Lincoln's insistence, were not harsh; and the tired, worn, valiant soldiers of the South were permitted to take home their horses or mules for the spring plowing. "Officers will retain their side arms." Strong men wept like April rain, and men in blue and men in gray embraced each other with relief.

The guns were silent; was it safe now to relax and rejoice? The more thoughtful, like Anne, wondered. The ordeal had been so long and so full of terrible anguish, "Ring out wild bells" in all the Northern cities, where people hoped that this might once again become the United States of America.

Important guests invited to see the minor English comedy play, *Our American Cousin,* in the Presidential box at Ford's Theater in Washington, on the night of April 14 had refused, each with his separate excuse. The excuse was probably just Mary Todd Lincoln, who had been almost insanely difficult of recent weeks, but they were too polite to touch upon that. General and Mrs. Grant had declined their invitation, and the Stantons couldn't make it. "Sorry, Mr. President. Some other time." Instead, Mr. and Mrs. Lincoln had for company only a romantic young couple, recently engaged, and an impersonal, ineffectual guard supposedly stationed at the doorway of the box, who decided rather to watch the play.

The Presidential box was pleasant, comfortable. Lincoln

enjoyed the theater and often attended, to rock to and fro in his special armchair and, unless he fell asleep from utter weariness, applaud the drama or the farce.

What happened that night is history. But at the moment Washington was rife with rumors and hysteria. Anne knew not what to think. It seemed that Lincoln had been shot by an erratic young actor named John Wilkes Booth, and there were rumors that the entire Lincoln Cabinet had been assassinated. All Washington was in a dither before the coming of the next dawn, while the President's life was slowly ebbing.

Slowly the facts emerged. Secretary Seward had been severely attacked as part of what was later shown to be a mass-murder plan. Anne and others had been spared this terroristic assault. But Abe Lincoln would not be at the helm of state any more; his gentle hand would not be there to guide the reconstruction and to weld the broken nation together. He was not to breathe the sweet air of peace, nor would he be there to stand firm and take care of unfinished business!

23

File for the Future

As Anne saw the cruelty and hatred suddenly released in Washington following Lincoln's death, there were times when she must have been faint at heart, wondering whether any of her work, her dedication to principles, had really been worth the effort. It was a period of severe disillusionment for her as for many others. They had fought to keep the United States of America whole and in one piece; but now, even with peace and victory, there seemed only chaos. Andrew Johnson, stepping into the Presidency, could not cope with the situation; perhaps even Lincoln could not have done so. Reconstruction had become retribution instead; the proud South must be made to pay and pay until its head was bowed.

Gone were her and Mr. Lincoln's high hopes for mercy, their plans for resettlement of the Negroes somewhere. The assassination had done the Republican radicals in Congress a double service; it had eliminated a strong, just, humanist President, and it had inflamed sentiment against the fallen Confederacy. It was not hard to make many thousands of people believe that Jefferson Davis and other Southern leaders had used John Wilkes Booth as their tool. The traitors must be punished   Meanwhile carpetbaggers invaded the stricken South, and above Mason and Dixon's line people sang, "So we'll hang Jeff Davis to a sour-apple tree. . . ."

Ulysses S. Grant might change all this, and Anne set out to back him. He was decent; he was honest; and he was being boomed for the Presidency. Anne had no reason to presume that he would not support her demand now for recognition and payment for her services to the nation. General Grant had never personally laid claim to the honor of creating the Tennessee strategy.

She was an idealist, but the times were materialistic. She had been patient far too long, and certainly she need be silent no longer for security reasons. She was sure that Lincoln would have spoken up stoutly for her had he lived, but she still had a strong coterie of prominent figures who were anxious to rally to her support. Stanton, before his own death, had said, "Her course was the most remarkable in the war. She got no pay, and did the great work that made others famous." As a mere woman, in a time when women had no vote and were considered second-class citizens, she had had to stand aside while others reaped the glory; but now she would step forward. It was a matter of principle to the fiery, brilliant redhead—and to those who wished to see justice done her and the truth come out.

Yet Anna Ella Carroll had not reckoned with the fact that she knew too much and had done too much where others had stumbled and failed. Grant was now being portrayed as an all-conquering Caesar; his war record would almost automatically elect him President, with offices to bestow upon the greedy thousands of his followers, who hastily climbed upon the bandwagon. Grant was suddenly almost godlike; biographers were already magnifying his image. As also with Lincoln then and ever since, biographers

187

and historians had discovered that they had a very good thing on which to build important reputations for themselves. Why disturb the growing myth? They preferred to ignore the simple truth soon to be recorded in a stack of documents in the Library of Congress, in leading magazines, such as the *Century, Godey's,* and *North American Review,* and in a two-volume biography of Anne herself, written and largely published during her lifetime. As a matter of historical justice, one has only to suggest that these be examined; they are impressive and they speak for themselves—and for Anne. They speak as clearly and forcibly today, when resurrected from the files, as they did in the time of Anna Ella Carroll. The published statements of such men as Benjamin F. Wade of Ohio, one of the most powerful men in the Senate all through the war:

I cannot take leave of public life [he wrote Anne] without expressing my deep sense of your services to the country during the whole period of our national troubles. Although a citizen of a State almost unanimously disloyal and deeply sympathizing with secession, especially the wealthy and aristocratical class of her people, to which you belonged, yet, in the midst of such surroundings, you emancipated your own slaves at a great sacrifice of personal interest, and with your powerful pen defended the cause of Union and loyalty as ably and effectively as it has ever been defended. . . . From my position on the Committee on the Conduct of the War, I know that some of the most successful expeditions of the war were suggested by you, among which I might instance the expedition up the Tennessee River.

Wade was incensed on Anne's behalf, and after returning to Washington from Ohio, foregathered with Lemuel Evans and Thomas Scott to press her case before the Senate Committee on Military Affairs. They were going to insist that she be declared a major general, with full pay for that rank since November of 1861.

The fat was in the fire, to the embarrassment of the fervent partisans of Grant, who tried their best to make her claims sound absurd. The great hero of the war must remain high on his pedestal, and the public must continue to think that Grant had climbed there all by himself. Important public papers corroborating Anne's statements mysteriously disappeared from government files. Political Mumbo Jumbo and red tape must somehow keep this woman quiet!

It had been a man's war, and most officialdom would prefer to have forgotten the valiant assistance of the women. The ladies could not have the right to vote; but newly freed, illiterate Negro field hands had the right of suffrage. What utter nonsense that a woman should expect any recognition or reward, and how preposterous that any woman should be made a major general! Women were getting too big for their pantalettes!

Stanton and Attorney General Edward Bates were dead, but as Anne's other self-appointed knights fought her cause from various angles, she was herself preparing a voluminous statement of the whole story for presentation before the 42nd Congress. Called a *Memorial,* and amply documented, it was published on June 8, 1872.

It would seem impossible for legislators to pass lightly over the statements of men of such unquestioned integrity as those Anne quoted here: Edward Bates, Thomas Scott, the famous orator Edward Everett, the noted lawyer, Reverdy Johnson, Benjamin Wade, Lemuel Evans, now Chief Justice of the Supreme Court of Texas, and many other prominent figures. So Anne thought. To the unequivocal testimony of these eminent men, she added her own tactful note: "In preferring my claim to this, I cannot, by any possibility, detract from our brave and heroic commanders to whom the country owes so much; and, so far from opposing me, I believe that, as a class, they would be gratified to see me or anyone properly rewarded, according to the part performed in this mighty drama."

This *Memorial* was not the first of her requests but the most complete and incisive one; and the reaction to it was so favorable that final resolution of the problem seemed immediate. Senator Jacob M. Howard of Michigan, officially appointed to look into the whole affair, reported: "She did more for her country than all the military generals. She showed where to fight and how to strike the rebellion in the head, and also possessed judicial learning so comprehensive and concise in its style of argument that the government gladly sat at her feet to learn the wisdom of its powers."

Once her claims were settled, Anne would marry Lemuel Evans and go on a belated honeymoon. But it was not destined to be. Despite the weight of the evidence, the forces against Anne were cunning and shrewd. They were determined that Grant be reelected, even though the past four years of scandalous corruption in his administration had cast deep shadows upon him. He was not a fraud. Anne would have been one of the first to insist that he was not, but he was an innocent in politics and the dupe of scheming friends. The sensational press would seize upon any public recognition of Anna Ella Carroll's services to scream to the high heavens, "Grant is a fake; a woman planned all his strategy!"

In consequence of this situation, red herrings were drawn again and again across Anne's clear, true trail. The river pilot Scott was dug up to make an appearance and insist that all the glory of the Tennessee Plan should be his. The earlier enthusiasm for Anne's cause in Congress was replaced by portentous clearings of the throat, cold politeness, and again and again interminable delay.

No one had ever seriously refuted a single one of her claims. Not daring to face her openly, the scheming politicians of the Grant factions passed the cards from hand to hand beneath the table. With "the insolence of office" they conspired to let the passing of the months and years take care of her deeds and let them fade into oblivion.

They had not been forgotten by James A. Garfield. The Ohioans had always been intensely loyal to Anne since the days of Tom Corwin. And Garfield, once elected President, would make all right for her. But, as with Lincoln, Garfield was shot before he could take any real action. The imposing bill presented in Anne's behalf strangely disappeared before Congress could act upon it, and another took its place. It accorded her no honors, made no specific mention of her services, and curtly dismissed her with a paltry pension of $50 a month!

Anne's first impulse was to refuse it, to throw it back in their faces. And then she reconsidered. Her head was still high, but she had long been ill and now was living with her younger sister Mary, a government clerk.

They could never repay her for the services she had given so generously. And dollars could not buy her memories. Anne had a sense of history. She remembered the time long long ago when she had stood, as the Governor's daughter, in the old State House in Annapolis and wished that somehow she could play a vital role in the history of her country. It had seemed out of the question then, especially for a mere girl. Far-off dreams of George Washington and Thomas Jefferson and Carroll of Carrollton. And yet the dream had come true!

She had been able to bolster Governor Hicks and save Maryland for the Union, and with it undoubtedly the District of Columbia and the nation's Capital. She had, with her beloved nation drowning, been able to revive it with her Tennessee Plan and outline the ultimate source of victory.

In these later days of her life she had few regrets and many thoughts of gratitude. She had, indeed, lived tremendously. Many men had loved her; her deeply feminine heart had been gratified. She had stood by her family and her slaves; she had let no one down. None could despise her, and many could adore.

Above all, she had not lost her head amidst the tumult and the shouting. As Count Leo Tolstoy, the great Russian novelist and philosopher, wrote: "Life is a place of service, and in that service one has to suffer a great deal that is hard to bear, but more often experience a great deal of joy. But that joy can be real only if people look upon their lives as a service, and have a definite object in life outside themselves and their personal happiness." There was a good deal of all this in Anna Ella Carroll.

Her roots had been too deep in the East ever to leave it—even for Lemuel Evans. She had given her deepest devotion to her country in its direst hour of need.

Like the rivers she knew so well, she had carved her own channel. With a simple bouquet of violets in her still-beautiful hands and a smile lingering on her face, she lay forever quiet on February 19 of 1893.

Bibliography

Bates, Edward: *Diary,* Washington, Government Printing Office, 1933.

Beard, Charles A. and Mary R.: *The Rise of American Civilization,* New York, Macmillan, 1935, rev. ed.

Beirne, Francis W.: *The Amiable Baltimorians,* New York, Dutton, 1951.

Blackwell, Sarah E.: *A Military Genius, A Life of Anna Ella Carroll,* 2 vols., Washington, 1891–5.

Bradford, Gamaliel: *As God Made Them,* Boston, Houghton, 1929.

Carpenter, F. B.: *Six Months at the White House,* New York, Hurd, 1866.

Carroll, Anna Ella: Correspondence, personal and business. Letters on deposit with the Maryland Historical Society, Baltimore.

Carroll, Anna Ella: *The Great American Battle,* New York, 1856.

Carroll, Anna Ella: *Memorial to the 42nd Congress,* document in Library of Congress, Washington, 1872.

Carroll, Anna Ella: *Reply to the Speech of the Honorable J. C. Breckinridge,* pamphlet, Washington, 1861.

Carroll, Anna Ella: *Reply to Sumner,* pamphlet, Washington, 1861.

Carroll, Anna Ella: *Star of the West,* New York, 1857.

Carroll, Anna Ella: *The Tennessee Plan,* handwritten document in possession of Maryland Historical Society, Baltimore, November 30, 1861.

Carroll, Anna Ella: *The Tennessee River Campaign, North American Review,* April, 1886.

Carroll, Anna Ella: *The War Powers of the General Government,* pamphlet, Washington, 1861.

Century Magazine: *The Case of Miss Carroll,* August, 1890.

Chandler, Lucinda: *Anna Ella Carroll, the great unrecognized genius of the War of the Rebellion, Godey's* Magazine, September, 1896.

Dickens, Charles: *American Notes,* New York, Houghton, 1894.

Eaton, Clement: *A History of the Southern Confederacy,* New York, Macmillan, 1954.

Footner, Hulbert: *Rivers of the Eastern Shore,* New York, Farrar, 1944.

Grant, Ulysses S.: *Personal Memoirs,* 2 vols., New York, 1885.

Greenbie, Marjorie Barstow: *My Dear Lady,* New York, Whittlesey, 1940.

Greenbie, Sydney and Marjorie B.: *Anna Ella Carroll and Abraham Lincoln,* University of Tampa Press and Falmouth Publishing House, 1952.

Grierson, Frances: *The Valley of Shadows,* Boston, Houghton, 1948.

Groves, Ernest R.: *The American Woman,* New York, Greenberg, 1937.

Hart, Albert Bushnell: *Slavery and Abolition,* New York, Harper, 1906.

Johnson, Gerald W.: *America's Silver Age,* New York, Harper, 1939.

Jones, Elias: *Revised History of Dorchester County, Md.,* Baltimore, Read, 1925.

Kane, Harnett T., and Henry, Inez: *Spies for the Blue and the Gray,* New York, Hanover, 1954.

Keckley, Elizabeth: *Behind the Scenes,* New York, Carleton, 1868.

Leech, Margaret: *Reveille in Washington,* New York, Harper, 1959.

Lincoln, Abraham: *His Speeches and Writings,* ed. by Roy P. Basler, Cleveland, World, 1946.

Livermore, Mary A.: *My Story of the War,* Hartford, Worthington, 1888.

Maryland, a Guide to the Old Line State, compiled by workers of the Writers' Program, New York, Oxford, 1940.

National Cyclopedia of American Biography, New York, White, 1907.

Page, Thomas Nelson: *The Old South,* New York, Scribner, 1892.

Riddle, Albert Gallatin: *Recollections of War Times,* New York, Putnam, 1895.

Sandburg, Carl: *The War Years* (1939) and *The Prairie Years* (1926), 6 vols., New York, Harcourt.

Schurz, Carl: *Life of Henry Clay,* 2 vols., Boston, Houghton, 1887.

Stone, Irving: *Love Is Eternal:* Mary Todd and Abraham Lincoln, New York, Doubleday, 1954.

Todd, Helen: *A Man Named Grant,* New York, Houghton, 1940.

Trollope, Frances: *Domestic Manners of the Americans,* London, Whittaker, 1832.

Williams, T. Harry: *Lincoln and His Generals,* New York, Knopf, 1952.

Wilstach, Paul: *Tidewater Maryland,* Indianapolis, Bobbs-Merrill, 1931.

Woodard, W. E.: *Meet General Grant,* New York, Liveright, 1928.

WINIFRED E. WISE is best known as the author of the ever-popular *Jane Addams of Hull-House,* which has become a classic in its field, and *Rebel in Petticoats,* the story of Elizabeth Cady Stanton. Swimming in the Pacific surf and viewing the ocean floor through a face mask are favorite pursuits of the author. A graduate *cum laude* of the University of Wisconsin, she became a staff editor of *Compton's Pictured Encyclopedia* and has had a distinguished career in advertising as executive at Marshall Field & Company in Chicago, and J. W. Robinson, Los Angeles. She now lives in Laguna Beach, California, and is the wife of Stuart Palmer, well-known mystery writer. They have one daughter majoring in bacteriology at UCLA, another making recordings for RCA, and a son with the Air Force in France.